Understanding Preschoolers

Understanding Preschoolers

Anne Hitchcock Gilliland

Convention Press
Nashville, Tennessee

*Anne Hitchcock Gilliland is the mother of two children,
a conference leader, and a writer of Preschool materials.
She lives in Park Ridge, New Jersey.*

This book is the text for course number 6101 of subject area 61,
Understanding Work with Age Level and Special Groups in a Church,
of the New Church Study Course.

Library of Congress Catalog Card Number: 76-97867

Contents

Special for Readers!

Children under six are in the spotlight! They have the attention of today's world. Striking ideas in printed commercials penetrate the thoughts of the reading audience—"We're building our future for youngsters," "Meet one of our important customers," "You can raise your child's IQ," "Teach your two-year-old to read," "The kid-cushioned floor." Glance through any current secular magazine and note the many advertisements featuring preschoolers. Everything from the latest in scientific technology to the newest in soup flavors may be focused toward the child, even full-page, colored airline ads.

What does this emphasis on the child say to teachers and parents? It reveals that the commercial world is aware of an important aspect of today's society, that parents are interested in their preschoolers! Most parents understand what preschoolers need for good physical growth—nutritious food, plenty of sleep, cleanliness, appropriate exercise and play, and plenty of fresh air and sunshine. Generally, parents are eager to supply whatever is necessary for the physical and mental development of their preschoolers, but needs are much deeper than just the physical and mental.

In recent years, through study and research, tremendous advances have been made in the understanding of emotional needs and growth of preschoolers. All areas of growth are important in the development of a healthy personality—physical, mental, social, emotional, and spiritual—and one aspect of growth cannot be separated from another.

This book includes a variety of information that has been derived through study and research by specialists in various fields of early childhood. It will be useful to all adults who have association with preschoolers at home, church, nursery school, kindergarten, or other places.

This book presents the preschooler in today's world. It does not include the needs and abilities of every preschooler; that would be impossible. But answers to some questions will be found: What is he like? What does he need? How does he learn? How does he grow spiritually? What makes one person different from another? How do adults affect a child's development? It is hoped that the study will be useful to teachers, parents, and other adults who want to gain more understanding, knowledge, and skill for the task of leading and guiding preschoolers.

Contents to Part I

The first five years of life are:

- a time of GROWTH
  From birth to school age, a child develops and changes more than during any other six-year period in his life.

Healthy, creative growth takes place in a friendly environment.

- a time of PERSONALITY development
  A person's basic personality and character are formed in the first five years of life.

My name is Steve. I am an important person.

- a time of LEARNING
  Some research indicates that by age six a child has learned half of what he will know at maturity.

How does a child learn to speak a language?

Part I

The Preschooler Is a Person

1. WHO IS THE PRESCHOOLER?

The tiny baby—helpless without our love and care.
The creeper—constantly on the move!
The toddler—reaching out to taste, to touch, to feel,
    to squeeze.
The two-year-old—"on the go" and "no-no" stage.
The three-year-old—"I can do it myself!"
The four-year-old—"I have an idea!"
The five-year-old—"I *want* to please you; I really do."

and

On toward six—"I'm active and noisy, but I want to go
    to school."

Each child is a person—different from every other human
being. Each child is a growing personality.

In a sense, each child builds his own world.

"The unfolding of personality cannot be arranged, it cannot be forced into a convenient or efficient time schedule."[1]

". . . Personality develops as a result of a constant interaction between the child with his unique way of reacting, and his total environment, in which his parents are highly influential elements."[2]

Who can be sure what a child is like until he has observed him in many activities over a period of time?

---

2. WHAT CAN ADULTS LEARN ABOUT PRESCHOOLERS?

Some preschoolers are sensitive.
Others can sleep through a houseful of guests.
Some babies cry when bathed.
Others splash, kick, and coo in water.
What makes such differences in individuals?

Through many ages, two philosophies of developmental differences have prevailed. The *constitutionalist* view declares that differences exist because of characteristics present at birth, presumably inherited. The *environmentalist* view maintains that differences occur due to the influence of environment and experience.

With the advances in science and technology during the nineteenth and twentieth centuries, man has not been satisfied with the ancient views in developmental differences. Three studies, in particular, during the twentieth century have enriched our understanding of child development and behavior.

Sigmund Freud, in his study of the effect of environment on child development, gave insights into the emotional and motivational factors as influenced by parent-child relationships.

Dr. Arnold Gesell, in study and research of behavior at various age levels, found that physiological and social behavior follow clear developmental sequences. Being aware of the developmental levels helps adults understand each child more thoroughly.

Jean Piaget's work on thought processes of young children may be summarized. The child's growth in thinking ability takes place in stages that can be identified by his achievements. Each stage prepares the way for the stage that follows it. The first stage of sensorimotor intelligence lasts 18 months or more.[3] The infant and young toddler come to know their immediate environment as permanent objects and background, separate from themselves.

"The stage of preoperational thought . . . begins at around 18 months or two years and ends at around seven. During these years, the child becomes less egocentric as his thought processes become more flexible, more controlled and less dominated by his perception and his wishes." [4]

Continued study has not bypassed all that has been learned about what causes growth and what forces influence differences in all living things. Recent research indicates that physical growth and development is an interaction between inborn factors and environment. Nature (heredity) and nurture (environment) are two sets of forces constantly influencing each other. Development is, therefore, the product of the interaction of both sets of forces.

Thus, one person is different from all other persons because of *nature* and *nurture*.

How a person *feels* is equally as important as what he *knows*.

---

3. HOW CAN PRESCHOOLERS BE UNDERSTOOD?

It is not easy to understand preschoolers. We cannot always interpret the reason for a child's behavior. Sometimes we make mistakes in guidance. But children need adults who *want* to understand them, who keep on trying to learn ways to help them.

Parents and teachers must have confidence in their own good judgment and sense of trust so that they may guide children in ways that will help each one according to his needs. Adults must be able to trust their ability to make right decisions about preschoolers. This comes from developing wholesome values, observing other parents, studying, using common sense, and continuing practices.

Preschoolers Need Adults Who Understand Them—

• Who accept the fact that no two individuals are alike. Each child must be guided according to his personal temperament and needs.

• Who are aware of general growth patterns, personality development, and developmental changes at various ages and stages. A mother who knows that preschoolers have a decline in appetite when they are nearing two years of age will not worry and fret when Jimmy, at nineteen months, seems to have lost his keen interest in food. A four-year-old is no longer just exploring and manipulating materials; he often has an idea in mind and reveals it in words, through art, or through other actions.

• Who accept behavior with awareness and understanding, encouraging change in desirable directions.

• Who give children opportunity to express their feelings and thoughts. During Sunday School, Mrs. King allowed five-year-old Anita to tell about her trip to her grandfather's farm, even though it meant there was not time to play the game Mrs. King had planned to use.

• Who have understanding and faith in the fact that there is value and power in nonverbal (relationship) teaching. A father and his son see a blind man sitting by a building as they pass. The father places some money in the basket beside the blind man. The five-year-old looks, pulls a nickel from his pocket, and drops it in. The daddy smiles at his son; no word is spoken.

Being two or four or six makes a difference in behavior.

WAYS FOR ADULTS TO GROW IN UNDERSTANDING PRESCHOOLERS

1. Read books, newspaper columns, pamphlets, and magazine articles about child development. A helpful list of books and pamphlets may be found in the Resource Materials on pages 158–163.

A study of *Preschoolers at Church* by Chamberlain, Harty, and Adams and *Guiding Preschoolers* by Hearn is necessary for

an overall look at the child under six and the Preschool program.

2. Learn *with* preschoolers as you guide them at home, church, nursery school, kindergarten, or as you have other associations with them. Give attention to adult-child relationship as well as child behavior. Many teachers are quick to observe the difference in behavior of children on Sunday morning and Sunday evening.

3. Observe preschoolers in natural situations, as they have freedom in following their own interests (perhaps a few preschoolers playing together outdoors).

4. Observe different groups of preschoolers—ethnic groups, rural, urban, underprivileged—to learn how they act in various settings and circumstances.

5. Attend public meetings, such as school functions, to hear preschool specialists, to see films, or to participate in discussions related to child development. Participate in local, associational, **state, and convention conferences planned in the interest of** preschoolers.

6. Talk with people who have a deep understanding of preschoolers—a more experienced teacher at church, a nursery school or kindergarten teacher, a college teacher of early child-

Merrill Moore

hood education, a librarian, or a pediatrician.

7. Make written records of behavior and other observations of a child at the time of happening. Write down what the child actually does, what he says, how he acts, and the adults' reactions to the child (not what you think he does or says, or how he acts). Such records can be useful over a period of time in helping a parent or teacher understand a child's behavior and development.

Records on individual child behavior in a church department are good resource material for workers in evaluating progress and needs of each child. The records are also a guide for determining purposes and goals and for planning department procedure. The records can give adults insight into ways they need to improve adult-child relationships.

In departments for three-, four-, or five-year-olds, one worker may record experiences which occur during a group time. Such notes, taken over a period of several weeks, can capture for the adults ideas, expressed emotions, exact language, apparent fears, conflicts, concepts, and attitudes of preschoolers.

One educator suggests that "studying young children can be an excellent way to understand all human behavior."[5]

Since each child is unique, adults have the responsibility to respond differently to each child. Too often they are treated alike as if they all have the same abilities and needs.

- How do you react to the child who is shy and does not reply when you speak to him?
- What is your response to a friendly child?
- How do you act toward the child who consistently cries when he does not get his way?

Adults have in their minds "images" of preschoolers and their behavior. One's image of a particular child may interfere with giving the kind of guidance needed at a particular time.

Adults often have such images as the following about children:

spoiled	cry baby	noisy	cute	naughty
bad	stupid	good	selfish	quiet

Two adults observe a child engulfed in tears. One adult sees the child as lonely; the other views him as "just a crybaby." Each adult's reaction to the child will differ because of his concept.

It is important that teachers and parents who guide children see each child as he really is, for the adult's response to the child will have a strong influence on the child's behavior.

A child's behavior reflects the way his mother and father handle their parental roles.

ANALYZING WHAT ADULTS OBSERVE

It takes practice to learn to observe what is really happening in a preschooler's experience. An observer must give careful attention to details:

What is the child feeling?
What is the child thinking?
How is the child reacting toward other children?

How is the child responding to an adult in his environment?
What do children seem to need from adults?
How does the child treat the *things* in his environment?
What are individual children's interests?
Does the child assume appropriate responsibility?

An observer must look at each preschooler as he really is, hearing the words a child actually says and seeing what he actually does. An adult's "image" of a specific child or children in general may influence what he sees. The adult may not see what actually happens because of what he anticipates seeing. Behavior may be quite different from what it appears to be. Four-year-old Jim was sitting in a chair near the door in the department. When asked by an incoming teacher why he was sitting there, he said: "They're making me sit here 'cause I kicked Jeff. But he kicked me first like this." Because of Jim's aggressiveness, a teacher assumed (even though he didn't see the hitting) that Jeff was the initiator of every scuffle in which Jim was involved.

While observing, it is helpful to take written notes of specific actions, words, and other details. One may gain more insight or get a different view about what really happened as he analyzes his notes on observation.

Adults must train themselves to observe details—not just describe in a general way what they *think* is happening.

WHY PRESCHOOLERS DIFFER

Preschoolers differ because of what they inherit from their parents and because of the effects of their environment and experiences beginning at birth. Growth and development take place through the interaction of heredity and environment (nature and nurture) within an individual.

What does an individual inherit? The factors which rank high are: eye color, complexion, body build, intelligence, and talents (music, art). Heredity influences how tall a person can become under normal growth and development. Inherited characteristics include such things as speed of reaction, sensitivity to sound or light, and intensity of response. However, there are opportunities for changes in many areas because of the interaction between hereditary and environmental forces.

Some environmental influences on development:

1. Kind of care that parents (or parent substitutes) give the child (firm discipline, allowance for choices, variety of foods)
2. Personal relationship between parents (consideration, love, kindness, gentleness)
3. Family values (faith in others, importance of church-going)
4. Exposure to different sights and sounds (varying experiences with things in the natural world)
5. Exposure to climate (awareness of cold, cool, and warm weather; rain; snow)

WHY THE SAME PRESCHOOLER ACTS DIFFERENTLY AT TIMES

Circumstances often contribute to a child's behavior. A child who is normally happy in his room at church on Sunday morning may cry most of the time on Sunday night? Why? Often such behavior is caused because the child is tired and sleepy, perhaps even hungry.

Usually, the child whose behavior is out of character for him has a problem and needs understanding and comfort. A child may be ill, lonely, afraid, confused, or unhappy. He may be in a situation in which he does not know what is expected of him.

The same child also develops different behavior patterns as he goes through stages of development. In each phase, behavior is different. A problem, such as fear of strangers, may have different meanings at various stages of development.

WHY PEOPLE CHANGE

Within all living things is a strong impulse to grow and change. As the forces of life interact within an individual, his personality begins to unfold. Behavior patterns change as a child grows out of one age and stage into another.

A child changes because someone loves and cares for him or because he feels alone, unloved, and rejected. The child who feels he is loved will tend to do that which is acceptable to the one who loves him. He is not afraid of change. The child who is not

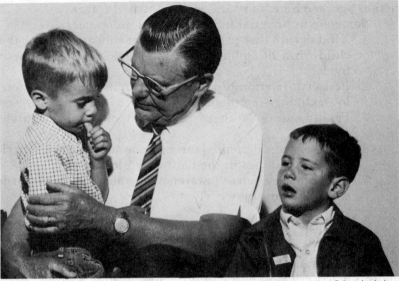

Robert L. Jackson

accepted for what he is grows more hostile and reacts with unacceptable behavior.

The following adaption from James L. Hymes, Jr. is expressive of how children feel about themselves and reveals to adults a child's desire for growth and independence.[6]

> The child is the pusher—
> He *wants* to grow!
>> I want to grow up!
>> I want to be big!
>> Me do it!
>> I'm old enough.
>> I'm big enough.
>> Let me try!
>> I'll answer it.
>> I'll carry it.
> Why can't I?

Each child produces an effect on his world as well as the world producing an effect upon him.

---

4. WHAT ARE THE BASIC NEEDS OF PRESCHOOLERS?

The basic needs of children as set forth in this section have been adapted from the list presented in the book *A Parents' Guide to the Emotional Needs of Children* by Dr. David Goodman.[7]

LOVE

Psychologists agree that love is the child's first need. A child cannot be given too much love. Love is constant and continual, not something given as a reward for good conduct. Love is for "all the time." Love does not spoil the infant. Love comes from God and is channeled through parents and others to the child.

How does a baby know that he is loved? How do adults get the feeling across to him?

The atmosphere in the home tells the child when he is loved. A child needs harmony in the home. Parents must be happy, with themselves, with each other, and with members of the family. The baby needs parents who love and appreciate each other and love and appreciate him. In the home where parents have an overflow of mutual affection, the child finds comfort, security, and warmth.

A baby learns that he is loved through the simple, constant ministry to his needs. To a baby, food is love. It is important to help him discover that the world he has entered is a place where he can be satisfied—where he will be cared for and his needs will be met. The infant who is fed when he is hungry; who is kept clean, warm, and comfortable; who is cuddled when he needs attention; and who has adequate rest and sleep will gradually build a sense of security inside himself—a satisfaction that he is loved and wanted.

Babies know when they are loved or rejected.

Nothing can take the place of the love parents show a child by their joy and delight in relationship with him. Love is basic in a child's spiritual growth. Dr. Goodman says: "Your baby's exchange of smiles with you is his first lesson in love. . . . Your

Every Child Needs

Love

Guidance   Acceptance

Control   Security

Dependence   Sense of Trust
and
Independence

Self-respect

child has made his first great step in spiritual growth when he smiled back at your smile. He has learned life's most necessary lesson, how to give as well as receive love."[8]

It is through a parent's love that a child begins to develop a conscience. A child learns from his surroundings about acts that are acceptable and unacceptable. These learnings become a part of him. By loving a child enough to let him know how you feel about things, what is important, to you, and what you think is right and wrong—this is how conscience is developed.

The young child, feeling the love of his parents, learns to trust other adults. The loved child feels secure and happy in his church department when he senses that the teachers there love and care for him.

How a child feels toward people throughout life will depend to a great extent on how he felt in the early years of life: the world is a friendly place or a dangerous one.

The child's feeling that he is loved is the foundation upon which he develops love toward other people. As the child develops socially, he becomes aware of the needs and rights of others. How does a child *learn* to "love one another" (John 15:17)? Not by just *hearing* the words, not by just *saying* them—but through a continuing experience of being loved and loving.

The loved child has a comfortable security, but an unloved child may go through life burdened with doubts and fears. What can teachers do for the child who comes to the church department feeling unloved? Teachers can love him. They can let him know

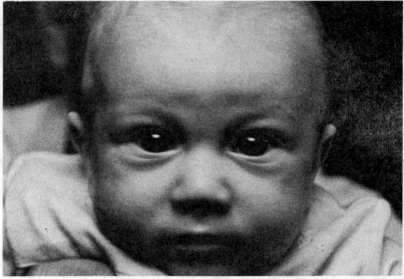

Wallowitch

he is loved. They can smile their warmth of understanding. They care for his physical and emotional needs. They provide opportunities for him to interact with other children and adults. Teachers help him feel he is as important as every other child in the room.

Loving care is the best insurance a child can have against developing crippling anxieties.

ACCEPTANCE

The child needs to feel that parents and other adults like him just the way he is. The child wants to be accepted *all* the time, even when parents or teachers do not approve of his behavior. As he continues to feel loved and accepted, he develops the ability and desire to respond in obedience to adult guidance (provided it is not too rigid). The well-loved child is stabilized in personality.

Rigid rules, enforced contrary to the child's needs or individual temperament, cause him to feel rejected. Toilet training, eating, and sleeping are areas of development in which adults often fail to consider each child's temperament. It is important to work *with* the child, not against him. Accept the child's natural body rhythms. Strive toward making him comfortable and physically satisfied.

A child who is loved and accepted for himself—not what he does—feels valued as a person. The feeling that he is acceptable to God at all times can also be a powerful force in each child's life. A parent or teacher who says, "God won't love you if you do that," is speaking untruthfully. An unthinking mother may say, "Put your toys away if you want Mother to love you." What? Withhold love to get obedience? The child needs the love of a parent or other adult friend as a free expression of feelings, not on condition. A child who is loved for being himself will gain self-confidence. The child who has to *earn* acceptance feels unworthy. His feelings may result in rebellion and aggression or submissiveness. If so, such behavior is his attempt to attract attention to his need for acceptance.

A child who is rejected, displaced, or otherwise not accepted may have difficulty developing a conscience (see pp. 125–126). Many adults in today's society feel that they are plagued by the undesirable behavior of children. If all children received adequate love and acceptance, reinforced by good examples in adults, each would develop a conscience that would call forth responses of desirable conduct.

Teachers may have a part in inspiring and influencing when they have affection and worthy regard for a child who comes from a home where he is rejected. Using special ways to praise a child helps a child feel more accepted.

William W. Russell

Ask yourself—
Do I *really* accept each child as he is?
Are my standards too high?
Do I expect too much?
Do I take my feelings of frustration out on the child?

SECURITY

A child must feel safe—assured that he is physically and emotionally secure. A child does not feel safe in an environment where he senses there is no control—where "the sky is the limit." Preschoolers want adults who set bounds that protect them from the onslaughts of others and from their own lack of control. The feeling that God is in control of the world helps a child develop a sense of security.

Preschoolers want happiness, control, and understanding among family members. They want *parents* more than *things*. In a home where there is a sense of security, children are likely to be considerate of each other and cooperative in family matters.

Harold M. Lambert

This principle applies to the child's feelings when he is in church, school, or other surroundings.

Parents and teachers in America want their children to have the best; the trouble is that adults are better at giving *things* than giving themselves. Children need time, companionship, and a personal relationship with parents and other adults who are responsible for guiding them. There is no real security in *things!*

Children prefer high standards of conduct, provided they are practiced by the adults. Children are loyal to adults who train them in ethical ways, for this indicates real care and interest.

Courtesy has deep roots, and is more likely to be *caught* than *taught*. A child needs to hear polite remarks. He soon follows an adult's pattern. A child who is treated courteously by his parents and other adults feels secure about his worth.

Unfortunately, it is easy for courtesy to be displaced by a spirit of irritability, especially toward children. Adults, distressed by their own frustrations and anxieties, confront children with irritable words and deeds. Results? Children are made to feel insecure and inferior. Use positive, happy, cheerful, hopeful, trusting words. These words will stimulate the child toward growth and personality development.

Security, understanding, and courtesy—these give a spiritual quality in the home and the church that children remember.

A child must feel safe—sure of love from others.

SENSE OF TRUST

A person cannot relate to Jesus if he cannot first trust himself, his environment, and people whom he knows best. As a child develops a sense of trust in the adults who care for him, a foundation is being laid for him to develop faith in the God who created him.

If parents and other adults are to help the child develop a sense of trust, they must have real faith in spiritual values—a faith that gives inner poise and self-confidence. The adult who feels that he is living in accord with God's purpose will have peace of mind and heart, for his faith establishes a positive attitude of mind.

Parents are the strongest influence in their child's religious life.

Faith is a very real and practical force. Though the young child does not understand faith, he senses it. Most preschoolers who live with adults who have Christian faith are likely to face life with a foundation for deep moral values. Adults in the home and church must communicate by example such attitudes of confidence, affection, concern for others, love, and goodwill toward others.

Simple, routine things in adult-child relationships help a child develop a sense of trust:

- Listening with interest to what a child has to tell.
- Talking over the child's problem and helping him reach a solution.
- Giving correct answers to his questions.
- Keeping the secret which he shares.

- Keeping the promise made to him.
- Admitting a mistake when it is made.
- Being fair in the guidance of child-to-child relationships. Avoiding making hasty decisions or judgments in matters where all the facts are not given.
- Expressing appreciation for kind actions a child performs for you, even though they are crude according to adult standards.

A parent should not leave the child without telling the child that he is going.

SELF-RESPECT

Various terms are used in reference to a person's feelings about himself: Self-image, self-concept, self-esteem, and self-respect are commonly used. Out of self-respect, a child develops self-confidence and becomes a responsible individual.

The kind of self-image a child develops is dependent upon his experiences of love, acceptance, security, and a feeling of belonging. When helped to develop a feeling of self-respect he feels at ease, joyous, and a cooperative member of a family or group. A child who feels rejected, unloved, and insecure views himself as being of little value to those around him. He tends to act the way he feels others expect him to act. If a child feels that people expect him to whine and beg for things he wants, he will continue to whine and beg. Without self-respect, an individual lacks the capacity to develop appreciation and esteem for others.

Parents and teachers need to help each child recognize his personal rights and his dignity as an individual just as they guide him to realize the rights and dignity of others. As adults sense God's value of the individual, a child is strengthened within.

Every child needs reassurance about his worth as an individual.

By the age of three, a child usually has a good idea about what his parents and other people whom he knows expect of him. The child's tendency is to *be* what others, especially his parents, think him to be. If he conceives that they look upon him as a tyrant, he will be a tyrant. If he feels he is loved, he will love.

A child tends to see himself as he feels his parents see him.

Acceptance of self does not imply that an individual, even a four- or five-year-old, is completely satisfied with himself as he is. A child may be striving to change a behavior pattern which he knows his parents or other adults do not approve. And he is not likely to berate himself while he is trying to change if the adults who are important to him continue to accept him.

A child's self-respect will affect how he feels about others.

DEPENDENCE AND INDEPENDENCE

A child needs to feel protection, to know there is an adult nearby on whom he can depend when a situation is beyond his abilities. Before a child can achieve independence, he must experience protection and security.

A child needs to feel there are certain things that he can do because he has reached the appropriate stage in his development for that degree of independence. However, it is not wise that a child be given tasks for which he is not ready.

At home, church, or school, adults need to create an environment in which there is maintained for the child an adequate balance between dependence and independence. For example, in the child's room at church, materials should be arranged so that they are accessible to the children. A child is free to select and use materials that attract his interests. At the same time, if the child needs help in using supplies, he is secure in feeling that the adults in the room are ready to assist him with his needs. By the time a child is three, he enjoys having a rack at home placed low enough so that he can hang up his own clothes.

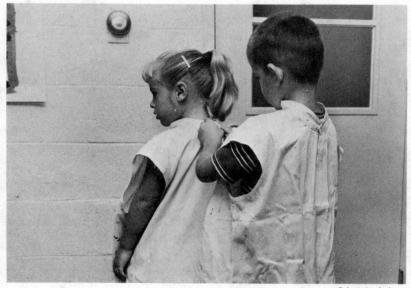

Robert L. Jackson

"Me do it!" "Let me do it!" are constant pleadings from the child who is eager to try out his abilities. The inner nature of the child is crying out for a chance to develop his independence! Do not rob the child of his tasks nor of his creativeness.

Give the child as much independence as he can handle. A child will show you, in word and action, how desperately he is striving to discover himself and his abilities. Avoid interfering with what a child is doing unless it is dangerous or destructive or infringes on the rights of others. Permit a child to work out his own problem whenever possible. Allow him to make some choices and decisions. Such opportunities help him grow stronger.

Does your church have hangers or hooks for preschoolers to use in hanging up their coats? If so, who hangs up the coat—parent, teacher, or child?

Many preschoolers suffer from overprotection. A child often develops fears and anxieties when adults try to shield him too closely. It is a mistake to try to live without problems or unpleasantness, for such a life does not exist. Help each child face problems as they come.

As a child develops independence, he also builds qualities for accepting responsibility.

It is difficult for a child to grow in independence
if adults do not allow him to assume responsibility
when he shows he is ready.

CONTROL

Consider the following statements and check any that you
think are true:

_____Appropriate discipline helps a child develop self-control.

_____Continual harsh punishment as a means of discipline may
cause a child to build inner hostility.

_____Discipline is a teaching-learning relationship between adult
and child.

_____The child who knows no limits is full of fears.

_____Constructive discipline is a sign of a parent's love and care.

Many educators today are declaring that one of the biggest
problems in the American classroom is *discipline*. Parents com-
plain that they have more trouble with discipline than anything
else. Church leaders are discouraged by the undesirable behavior
of children they are attempting to guide and teach.

Yet, almost any book on child behavior or child guidance
declares: Children want discipline. Children feel insecure in an
environment where there is no control. A child wants control
because he is afraid of his own impulses. A child who knows no
limits is full of fears.

Perhaps the question *"What is discipline?"* needs to be
asked. True discipline implies the *results* of learning in the life
of a child. Discipline is a teaching-learning relationship. The
adult disciplines the child, and the child becomes responsible
for his behavior. Ultimately, discipline is from within—it is a
matter of conscience. It is developing self-control. The instincts
to do right and wrong are both struggling within every person.
As adults consistently insist that a child do right, they encourage
the instinct for right. A child is not endowed with self-discipline,
but it can be developed over a period of time through careful
guidance by adults in whom the child trusts.

Can it be that one's fuzzy concepts about discipline have

hindered the confidence and ability to control children? How many adults identify punishment as the ultimate means of discipline?

Discipline—yes. But how do adults handle it?

Some adults approach children with an attitude of authority. Without consideration of the child's basic development needs or readiness for an experience, the adult approaches the child with a strict, rigid code of conduct. He attempts to gain control through threats and punishment. Specialists in child development and education contend that constant harsh punishment is not the answer to continued good behavior. Punishment may change behavior momentarily, but the change is usually temporary. Consequences of discipline by authority may mean: A child builds inner hatred, resentment, and rebellion that may come out later in attack on society; a child sees himself as inadequate and afraid to express himself; the child learns restraint *only with* authority; a child fails to develop self-control from within.

Other adults attempt to bring discipline into the child's life through a total permissive approach, also identified as the "indulgent" approach. In this experience, the child is free to explore his environment uninhibited—no controls, no direction as to the limitations society demands of him.

What are the results of "no control"? The child is confused; he feels uncertain of the love and care of adults; he is afraid; he has little regard for people or things.

A child *wants* and *needs* help in order to control his impulses. In an organized society, every child needs to develop self-control in order to survive.

A look at the child, as a person in the process of becoming mature, reveals him as one needing guidance and freedom measured to his level of development. Today a middle-of-the-road approach to discipline is often advocated, a balance between rigid authority and total permissive behavior. This is sometimes referred to as the developmental approach—freedom with control or freedom under guidance.

This approach to discipline is not easy. It requires patience, firmness in a friendly manner, understanding of children with individual differences, and consistent guidance.

This approach takes into consideration a child's need to assume some responsibility for his behavior at each level of development, and also the need for guidance in making decisions beyond his knowledge and experience. While control is maintained by adults, the child assumes control within his capabilities. Through this kind of adult-child relationship, the child learns self-control, which is true discipline.

In matters of discipline, ask yourself: "What is best for this child?"

Adults have more assurance in their ability to guide when they establish some principles in discipline, such as the following:

- Give the child love and understanding.
- Be consistent in what you expect a child to do.
- Be clear in your demands upon a child.
- Set only a few important rules.
- Try to prevent problems before they arise.
- Help a child understand the limits set up.
- Try to understand the reason for a child's behavior.
- Be a good example to children.
- Give praise when behavior merits it.
- Avoid blame that makes a child feel inadequate—an attack on him as a person.
- Use patience and self-control in insisting that rules be followed.
- Keep the child's temperament in mind.
- Think of discipline in positive terms.
- Remember that a child does not learn the first time.
- Give a child only the freedom he is ready to handle.

Then remember:
True discipline cannot be forced upon a child.

In discipline, the adult must like, respect, and want to help the child.

A child is not endowed with self-discipline. It can be developed over a period of time through careful guidance by adults in whom the child trusts.

Go back to the beginning of the section on discipline. Check your answers. How do they compare with what you have read? Do you feel you want to change any of your answers?

Wallowitch

GUIDANCE

Preschoolers need guidance in knowing how to get along in a world of people and things. No hard-and-fast set of rules can be made on *how* to guide preschoolers, but there are principles that may give the adult some direction:

- Be aware that each child's temperament and stage of development indicates the kind of help he requires at a given time.
- Know that what helps one child may not help another.
- Be consistent and explicit in what is expected of a child.
- Help a child experience success more often than failure.
- Keep the child within safe and acceptable limits.

There are specific areas of development in which a child needs guidance:

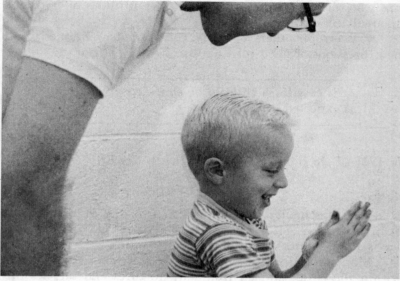

Du Puy

- He needs help in knowing how to be safe in a world of things—what is safe and acceptable to touch, to taste, to tear, to squeeze, to climb.
- He needs guidance in learning to relate to other people.
- He needs help when he attempts a task that is too difficult for him.
- He needs guidance when he misuses or abuses objects.
- He needs guidance in developing such skills as cutting with scissors, walking, or climbing.

The toddler does not understand about property rights— what is his and what belongs to another. Most two-year-olds are not ready to share. Most fives have developed some sharing ability as long as it is not having to give up his favorite possession. A wise adult may help a child who holds onto a prized toy to give up one of his toys, of less interest at the moment, to a playmate. This is one of the first steps in learning to relate to another. As a child develops interest in playing *with* another child (rather than alone or alongside a child), he will also develop a willingness to take turns and later to share.

If a child learns to relate to other persons, he needs grown-ups who set a good example—who show attitudes of faith and goodwill toward other people.

Concern for others, courtesy, compassion, and honesty may be expressions of one's spiritual life.

It is easy for a child to be confused about what is expected of him.

---

5. WHAT IS THE PRESCHOOLER LIKE?

THE PRESCHOOLER GROWS

The preschooler is an individual, growing in his own way at his own rate. Self-realization is the goal of his development. He is a personality—a thinking, feeling, acting individual.

Motivation for personal growth comes essentially from within the child, and environment nurtures and satisfies this motivation (or hinders or frustrates it at times). Growth is accounted for in terms of the interaction between hereditary and environmental forces.

In the modern approach to nurturing a child, the needs of the child are central. The degree to which the child's needs are achieved will determine the degree of personality development.

With the understanding of differences in individuals, a child may be thought of as "normal" in the sense that he is not handicapped in some way. Evaluation of a child's development emphasizes individual differences, with respect for his individual growth pattern as opposed to a simple comparison of the child's progress with averages of the population. Growth toward becoming a mature person has no timetable that operates with absolute regularity for each child. In Christian ministry, it is important to be informed on the general process of human development, for one must be aware of the stage a child has reached in order to nurture his growth.

A child's growth is not caused by other people or the world in general, but it is stimulated and influenced by them.

Through extensive research and study on child development, Arnold Gesell and his associates have provided a gauge for the rate of an individual's growth and also give insights into the readiness in a child.

The description of typical behavior for age and stage was not designed to show how children are alike, but to help adults see more clearly the differences. This approach helps adults know that a child may not be equally advanced in all aspects of growth. For example, his degree of emotional maturity may lag behind his physical growth; his language growth may come slower than his social growth.

Several principles regarding growth are important to understanding and guiding preschoolers:

- The child wants to grow.
- There is law and coherence in human development.
- Growth and development proceed in orderly fashion and have direction.
- Growth is uneven.

Pine Lake Farm

- Each stage is an outgrowth of the one preceding it.
- There is sequence in development.
- Experiences appropriate to his level of readiness are necessary for each child.
- A child proceeds from one stage to the next.

Considerations of development in this section pinpoint general growth patterns and growth changes, individual differences, characteristic emotional behavior, and developmental tasks at various stages.

A child develops faster during the years from birth to six than during any other five or six years of his life.

Growth patterns and growth changes.—At six months an infant cannot talk; at twelve months or soon afterwards, he can say one or two words. Why the change? He has arrived at mental maturity necessary for language development. Just so, a child does not walk until the development of the muscles for walking is reached, regardless of the amount of coaching he may have. A child of five does not retell a story at length until he has learned to associate the story he tells with his past experiences. This concept of "readiness" emphasizes that a child becomes capable through *maturation*. Growth changes occur as a child passes from one stage to the next.

Individual differences.—Certain behavior patterns are present at birth. These are evident early in infancy. The following are some behavior styles that make one person different from another:

- Degrees of interest in the environment.
- Sleeping rhythms—amount and depth of sleep needed.
- Level of sensory sensitivity (the sensitive one who cries the moment he is soiled).
- Intensity of response (a baby's cries are loud and piercing when he is hungry).
- Activity level (some more active than others).

Emotional behavior.—Emotions form a basic part of everyday life. Emotional behavior involves feelings, physiological changes, and behavior patterns. Emotions are more difficult to understand than other growth areas because one cannot see emotions. The emotional climate of the home is dependent upon the parents. The emotional climate of the child's room at church is dependent upon the teachers.

Behavior patterns of emotions can be recognized by such responses as crying, laughing, frowning, fighting, moods, or silly behavior.

Emotions at first are vague. Emotional behavior is unstable during infancy. A child may go from one emotional state to another very suddenly, with intensity and brevity. As a child learns gradual control and wholesome use of his emotions, he is able to accept himself and others in a satisfying way.

BABIES AND CREEPERS

All in all, babies are sturdy, but their very nature demands that they must be loved. Without loving care, a baby's whole growing-learning process may tumble. A baby learns through feeling. He learns to trust or mistrust. He learns to respond in

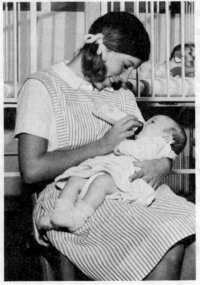

J. Carey Wood

It is hard for adults to recapture the helplessness of infancy.

love or fear, depending on the nurture he receives in the beginning stages of life.

The Newborn

In spite of his helplessness, the baby is born with instinctive abilities that cause him to carry out actions that are necessary for survival. He can:

Blink his eyes	Grasp with his hand
Cough and sneeze	Swallow
Yawn	Urinate
Cry for help	Defecate
Suck	Sleep

Birth is probably the most disturbing experience, relative to strength of personality, that a newborn undergoes. It is certainly the first big challenge that comes to a baby.

Development of senses.—At birth the infant has visual sensitivity but not discrimination of objects. It will be many weeks before he uses his eyes effectively. He is sensitive to touch. The mouth is the most sensitive organ at first. The sense of smell is significant. His hearing is well developed. Then comes feeling.

Response.—The newborn's characteristic emotional behavior is excitement. He is impulsive and responds to whatever stimulates him, like temperature changes, a loud noise, or bright lights. But stimuli from within—feelings of hunger, thirst, pain, or discomfort—are more likely to call forth response.

The newborn may have a reddish, wrinkled skin which soon takes on the normal color. His head is large in proportion to the size of his body. His arms are longer than his legs. His fingers are short. He breathes in a somewhat rapid and irregular way. His temperature-regulating mechanism is poor, so he gets hot or chilled quickly. He cannot control the movements of his head.

Growth.—A healthy baby sleeps most of the time, waking only to be fed or made comfortable. He is helpless and dependent upon others for his every need. It is important to help the newborn find that the world he has just entered is a place where he will be cared for and his needs satisfied.

Babies Grow

By the end of the *first month,* the infant can hold up his

head. He looks straight ahead when lying on his stomach. Sometimes within the first *three or four months,* he can hold his head up when his mother holds him on her shoulder.

Gradually, the baby develops control of his eyes. By *two or three months,* he can see a rattle or other object held above him. His whole body goes into motion reaching for the object. By about the *fourth month,* the baby's arms come up for the object and his hands clumsily grasp it.

Within the *first three to four months,* the infant develops a social awareness of the one who is caring for him. He may distinguish his mother from other persons. Verbal expressions have little meaning for the young baby, but he becomes aware of the person's feel. Touch is important to him. Hands and body speak the language of love that the infant can understand. The baby is searching for comfort and care. He begins to develop trust—or mistrust—through the feel of the hands and body ministering to him. "Its foundations are laid in the very first year of an individual's life." [9]

During this period, the infant has capacity to develop emotional distress, which he may experience if his needs are con-

stantly and continually neglected. Such experience can seriously impair his development in feeling comfortable, loved, and secure.

Feeding is one of the experiences in which the baby has the body contact that helps him feel safe and content. Even when he is getting milk from a bottle, the baby establishes ideas about the world through his feelings while he is held to be fed.

In the *early months,* a baby finds it almost unbearable, when he is hungry, to have to wait to be fed. If he is fed when he is hungry, he gradually regulates himself to fit into the routines of family living. He finds it easier to wait when he has come to feel safe and sure that his needs will be met.

In the period *two through four months,* the infant begins to make gurgling noises, coos, and babbles. Around *four months,* his cooing may be a response to other persons' sounds, presence, or attention; or to music or other sounds.

A healthy baby gains weight rapidly in the early months. By the end of *five months,* he may have doubled his birth weight. In these early months, he may grow as much as four inches in length. Around *five months,* a baby may start turning himself over—the beginning of mobility.

Around *six months,* an infant may become shy or afraid of strangers. He may fear unfamiliar objects or situations, loud or unfamiliar noises, or pain. He has the capacity to experience emotions of anger or disgust.

A baby is fortunate if he has relationships with other children. By *six months,* he is likely to respond in delight to associations of another child. Brothers and sisters are a help to a baby in developing his ideas about himself and others. Other children in the family may be a means of understanding that a baby not only is influenced by his environment, but that he also exerts influence on the world. This influence is evident when other children in the family respond with the emotion of jealousy toward a baby.

Within the time of *four to six months,* an infant can lift his head and chest when he is placed on his stomach. About midyear, a baby usually sits up when he is placed in a sitting position. Some babies begin to crawl at six months, perhaps backward as much as forward.

From *six to seven months,* a baby may vocalize several defined syllables. By *nine months,* he may imitate sounds he hears others make.

**Verbal expressions mean little to the very young.
Hands and body speak to him.**

A remarkable achievement occurs somewhere in the period of *six to twelve months.* This is the capacity to bring together in "pincer grip" the thumb and forefinger. Dr. Hymes acknowledged this accomplishment as "a major landmark in our development as humans." [10] The baby uses one arm, one hand, and a thumb and forefinger to grasp the object and release it. He can pick up even small objects with this technique.

J. Carey Wood

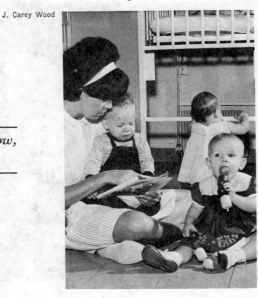

**"If I can't be a baby *now,*
when can I be?"**

From *seven or eight months to one year,* there are visible and steady changes in development:

The baby can sit upright for a time without fatigue.
The baby crawls.
He pulls himself up.

To walk, he holds onto his crib or other furniture.

He stands alone.

He takes his first step.

He may duplicate such repetitious syllables as "Da-da" and "Ma-ma."

He may experience fear of separation from his parents.

He enjoys a simple game with someone, like peekaboo. Play with a baby should be brief, for he tires easily.

He enjoys short, simple songs.

Before or after his *first birthday,* the infant may say his first word.

TODDLERS

Robert L. Jackson

He gets into everything!

The *toddler* is beginning to learn about the world. He is fascinated by things to touch, handle, poke, smell, hit, taste, or squeeze. This may include other children! The toddler's mouth is his main means of exploring his world.

The most important phase of development for the toddler is his major task in discovering that he is a person. He has a strong urge to be independent. His search for selfhood will continue on into the third year. It is necessary for him to feel that he is a person of worth in his growth toward selfhood. The kind of nurture the child receives from parents and other adults in his life is an important influence in his discovery of "Who am I?"

The toddler needs to feel safe and be safe through the care and guidance of friendly, helpful adults. He needs firm, gentle guidance.

This exploring toddler needs an environment that is safe and as free from strict regulations as possible, so that he is not in constant conflict with "Don't," "Mustn't," "No-no," "Hurt!" and hand-spankings. A mother is happier and more relaxed when the household detergents, medicines, and other potential "fatal" items are out of reach of the toddler. Why place a toddler in a room at church that is equipped to meet the needs of a four-year-old without expecting to have materials misused, scattered, and perhaps damaged?

Physical growth and motor control.—The second year is still a period of rapid physical growth. The child's body is changing, and he needs plenty of exercise. The toddler may be unsteady on his feet and likely to fall.

Some children, by sixteen months, have the ability to walk backward. By twenty months, a toddler may walk up and down a few stairs with help. In a few more months, he may walk the steps alone. By two years, many children walk well.

A toddler begins to develop some coordination of large muscles through climbing, pushing, and pulling. Finer muscles develop through feeding himself and manipulating toys that he can lift, drag, stack, and dump.

He's awkward with a spoon, but he learns by practice.

Some toddlers are not weaned. The age at which children are ready to be weaned varies, as it does with walking and talking.

Somewhere between one and two years, the child develops

a strong urge to feed himself. He will do a messy job at first, but he needs the opportunity to practice. He may continue for some time to use his fingers as a main "tool." Handling the food is his way to discover texture and temperature.

Most babies have a decline in appetite when they are nearing two years. A mother who is not aware that this is characteristic for the age may have conflicts with the child.

Toilet training.—Some parents take pride in seeing how early they can train their child in control of elimination. Unfortunately, the child may not be physically mature enough for control of bowel and bladder. Serious conflicts may develop between parent and child through the parent's insistent efforts at too-early toilet training. If a child resists, he should not be forced.

A child usually shows signs when he is ready for control. Watch for his interest in the bathroom, his inquisitiveness of family members' habits.

Toilet training is an important step in development—one more step for the toddler in gaining the independence he is seeking.

Language.—A toddler makes considerable growth in his ability to form words clearly during the second year. He is learning to combine sounds to make words.

During the second year, he often uses a single word to express a complete thought, which indicates more expression of emotion than naming an object. For example, "Doll" may mean "I want the doll" or "Where is the doll?"

By about twenty months, the child may combine several words to express a thought. As he approaches two years, the word No is more popular than Yes, for it is more expressive of self.

Emotional responses.—By toddler age, the child's capacity for emotional characteristics has broadened. He may show affection for adults and children; experience times of delight, elation, and excitement. He may also feel distress, fear, anger, or disgust.

The fear of being separated from his parents often is apparent when the child is brought to his department at church. An important principle to follow in helping the child overcome this fear is: Parents must not slip away from the child. This is more distressing to the child than the tears of saying good-bye. It does not contribute to his sense of well-being.

Social relationships.—The toddler is concerned mostly about himself. He has vague ideas about relationships with people.

To the toddler, other children fit into the same category as inanimate objects. Toddlers are seen poking, pinching, biting, hitting, and pushing in exploration of their environment.

A toddler does not know anything about property rights or sharing. He has to learn the idea of "mine" before he is ready to share with others. He likes to be near other children but does not know how to play with them.

Robert L. Jackson

The toddler is highly impulsive and goes overboard in using whatever is new. He explores and exploits the newfound possession.

He is beginning to want to do for himself—dress himself, feed himself, open objects. Through this "do for self" desire, the child begins to build strength and selfhood and power. But the letdown comes when he encounters experiences that "cut him down to size."

"Probably the most remarkable event in a child's life between the ages of one and three is that he learns to speak a language ... and we take this miracle completely for granted without ever really observing how it comes about." [11]

TWOS AND THREES

J. Carey Wood

The search continues! The two-year-old is still on his way toward independence—finding the answer to his one big question, "Who am I, really?" By two-and-a-half, his adventure is at its peak. He is in conflict with everything and everybody—whatever seems to be a hindrance to his independence. His most important (also most used) word is no!

What can adults do to stop such behavior, or should they try to stop it? It is at points like this that adults can gain help from study and research of specialists.

Studies reveal that the so-called problem behavior is normal at certain stages of development. We have learned that children revise behavior as they proceed from one stage to the next. Old problems tend to disappear as children develop.

However, it is important that adults accept the behavior as it occurs, learning to guide in ways that help a child feel good about himself. Recognize that the two-year-old is at an in-between stage—life for him is somewhat out of balance. The two has strong pulls from his baby world and a great impulse to be independent!

The two-year-old, though trying for independence, still needs an adult close by when he needs help. He is anxious to do for himself. "Me do it" is a favorite expression of this age. It is important to know a child's capabilities in order to allow him to do as much as possible for himself. At the same time, he does not need to experience too many failures.

The two-year-old begins to learn that everything has a name. He begins to realize that he can cope with the physical world, that he can manipulate objects mentally. His need to relate to the physical world may be experienced with building blocks or nature materials. He is learning to organize a part of his environment—testing out his ideas about what will work and what will not work. Painting, working puzzles, and modeling clay are efforts to recognize his world and make sense out of it. The child's natural urge to organize and make sense out of his object world is at the root of much of his most important learning.

A child is fortunate if he learns to feel that he is an important person.

By about three, a child senses his need to be all-powerful, to really discover *who he is*. The healthy three-year-old senses that he is *somebody*. He begins to look for new and different kinds of satisfactions.

Differences become more apparent in three-year-olds, particularly behavior patterns. A child may be friendly or unfriendly. The child develops behavior patterns to cope with his difficulties and characteristic ways of relating to situations.

Muscular development and coordination has its greatest gain in growth during the first three years. The following are **typical behavior characteristics** for twos and threes.

Characteristics generally evident in two-year-olds:

- Continues to be very active and likes to explore.
- Likes to feel, pat, and pound materials.
- Has a short attention span and his interests change rapidly from one experience to another.
- Responds to distraction, not to reasoning.
- Likes to play side by side (parallel play) by another child, but play is still mostly individual. His play is simple, mostly manipulative.
- Is developing a strong idea of "Mine," and does not understand sharing.
- Is beginning to ask questions about when, where, why.
- Has a vocabulary of about 300 words and uses short sentences (3 or 4 words).
- May have the capacity and interest to listen to a short story or a few words told about a picture or picture book. He delights in hearing brief, one-thought songs when they relate to himself or familiar experiences.
- May be interested in talking to God in his own way if the idea is suggested by an adult.

"I can't" may indicate that a child has not had sufficient chance to be independent.

Characteristics generally evident in three-year-olds:

- His physical appearance undergoes considerable change as his torso lengthens and he loses his baby chubbiness.
- He is beginning to have a vivid imagination. People and objects can become whatever he may imagine. He likes to pretend that he is someone else—doctor, fireman, policeman, baby, or daddy. His imagination can also contribute to emotional fear of "creatures."
- His growing body demands constant action. He walks and runs well, walks up and down steps alone, walks on tiptoes, and jumps with both feet. He needs play that helps develop control of large muscles.

• He is easier to control than two-year-olds; he responds more to reason. His ability to reason aids him in solving problems.

• He is developing a conscience, desiring to please those he loves and respects. Appropriate discipline is important toward the child's growth in self-control. He does not need to be made to feel ashamed or guilty beyond what he can handle.

A child's conscience begins to develop at about age three.

• He is learning to ask questions that provide him with information valuable to intellectual growth. He is literal minded and cannot interpret symbolic terms, such as "God's Word" (for Bible) or "God's House" (for church), or such songs as "This Little Light of Mine."

• He is imitative. Good examples in kindness, courtesy, and thoughtfulness are helpful.

• He is filled with wonder and asks many questions about things he hears and sees.

Pine Lake Farm

• Emotional feelings of anger or joy are strong. He needs firm and loving discipline to control his feelings. Some fears that are real to him are: dark, being alone, strange places, buildings, and animal noises.

Three-year-olds develop a sense of "Mine."
This is necessary before sharing can take place.

• He is beginning to enjoy contact and play with other children. As he learns to play with others, he develops an interest in taking turns and sharing.
• He can manage himself well in such tasks as dressing himself. He cannot tie a bow and may not be able to manipulate snaps, buttons, or zippers.
• He can accept some responsibilities, measured to his size, like putting toys away.
• He may enjoy informal experiences with music. He experiments with jingles and short tunes that he makes up. He likes to try out instruments like drums, rhythm sticks, triangles, or tambourines. His desire may lie in finding out what sounds he can produce from an instrument. A child may produce a rhythmic pattern as he experiments. Music should always be spontaneous for enjoyment at this age. He likes to listen to recordings, particularly activity records for his age.

A young child can find enjoyment in creating and singing his own songs.

• A three-year-old likes to hear stories. He wants to hear the same story or book many times if it interests him.
• A child who is regularly in church recognizes the Bible from other books in the room. He likes to turn the pages and look at pictures. He will listen briefly to a Bible story. He may be aware of some Bible thoughts and have a beginning concept of how to apply them. He is beginning to put into practice a few Bible principles, such as kindness and helpfulness.

FOURS AND FIVES

As preschoolers mature, the rate of growth is slowed. Hence

Bryce Finch

fours and fives show less differences in the kinds of activities in which they participate, but show greater skill in each activity.

During age three, the healthy child begins to look for a different kind of satisfaction in life—his *sense of initiative.* The four- or five-year-old is actively concerned with this same big task; he is eager to offer his ideas, try them out. He gains much through playing out experiences he has had.

Good discipline requires friendly firmness.

Readiness and maturation.—Readiness is a matter of maturation, and maturation cannot be forced. Readiness involves changes in muscles, bones, skeletal system, and nervous system which make it possible to acquire a skill.

A child usually practices skills for which he is ready. He is discouraged when he is urged to practice skills for which he is not ready. Fours and fives enjoy drawing or painting their own pictures on large sheets of paper (with large crayons or long-handled paintbrushes). A child this age may be frustrated if he is expected to color a picture within given lines (such as outline drawings and coloring books), for his coordination of finer muscles is not mature enough. He may, through effort, produce something that is fairly acceptable to adult standards, but this does not indicate that it was a good experience for him.

It is good to permit the child to experiment with cutting scraps of paper any way he chooses until he develops muscle coordination to cut with ease. Many fours do not have the skill to cut out an object with scissors, particularly if there are lines to follow.

If fours and fives spend too much time looking at small things or doing close work, they may develop nearsightedness.

In their eagerness to stop a child's play and continue formal learning, adults may expect more of fours and fives than preschoolers are ready to handle.

Physical and motor development.—Growth has a tendency to slow down in four- and five-year-olds. The child continues to have body changes as his torso, arms, and legs lengthen. Muscle tissues continue to develop and the child tends to tire easily.

The basic nature of the child's growing body demands a constant flow of activity. Fours and fives are generally interested in trying out all possible movements and manipulations of body. These actions contribute to muscular development and coordination. In the child's activity, his senses are constantly stimulated, and as a result he learns much.

These youngsters are extending body skills by running, walking, hopping, skipping, leaping, climbing, and balancing. Informal rhythmic responses to music also help the child improve motor control.

Fives can dress themselves; they may be able to tie a bow and manipulate buttons, snaps, and zippers. Many fours still need help with most of these skills.

They may improve small muscle coordination through working puzzles and pounding, pinching, squeezing, and rolling clay.

They move rapidly but do not like to be hurried. They tire from being inactive.

Social development and interests.—Fours and fives grow socially in many ways:

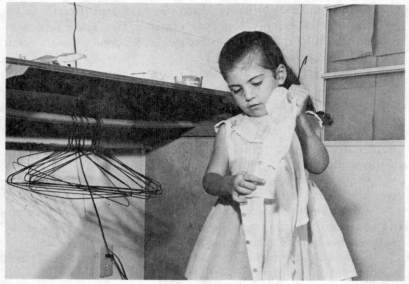

Bob Churchwell

• They grow in friendliness. Fives are more eager to get along with others.
• Fives are quite social. Fours enjoy playing in small groups with other preschoolers.
• Fives, particularly, are improving in ability to respect the rights and feelings of others.
• Fours and fives are learning to take turns and share; fives show more confidence in sharing.
• Fours have difficulty in sharing the attention of adults with other children.
• Fours seek adult approval; fives develop a growing dependence on other children their age.
• Fours and fives develop a concern and love for other people; fives demonstrate more interests in others.

Language and intellectual advances.—Fours and fives make a steady gain in language development. They can articulate words correctly and with meaning. Fives are especially concerned about the proper use of a word. The vocabulary of a five-year-old may be around two thousand words.

• The child's ability to think beyond the present is increasing. However, his concepts of time and space are very limited. A child may say "yesterday" in reference to an event that occurred a week or so before.

• Fives are better able than fours to comprehend verbal explanations. Comprehension of language is dependent upon past experience. The word "bulb" (in discussing planting flower bulbs) may be very misleading to the child whose mental picture is that of a light bulb. They interpret words literally and do not understand symbolic terms, such as "bread of life" or "the light of the world."

• Fours are curious and ask many "how" questions. Some fives are asking "why" questions.

• Fours enjoy looking at pictures and picture books, listening to recordings, and hearing stories read or told. Fives enjoy pictures, books, and music, but their attention span is longer.

Emotional characteristics and behavior.—Fours and fives show increasing control over their behavior if given good guidance.

• They respond to a great variety of stimuli in a fairly well

Pine Lake Farm

controlled manner. They feel secure in an environment where there is freedom with control. Fives express themselves freely if they have not been too inhibited.

• Expression of anger is probably the most commonly observed behavior, particularly with fours.

Children need experience in handling their own conflicts.

• Rivalry is more apt to appear at this age than jealousy.
• A sense of humor is often evident. Laughter accompanies play, even to becoming silly at times. They are easily amused by noises, someone falling, dramatic play, or the bumping and falling of children into each other.
• They may fear pain or physical harm. Hospitals, doctors, nurses, or instruments are associated with pain.
• Four-year-olds may develop many fears because of their active imagination.

Play patterns and interests.—Playing out their experiences is of great importance to fours and fives.

• Fours may plan ways to use materials, such as what they will build with blocks. Fives often plan with even more care. Fives usually decide what they are going to draw or paint before they use the materials.
• Children this age are not ready for games with rigid rules. They make up their own rules as they play and may change the rules during play. They may participate in a simple game initiated by an adult if there are only a few simple directions to follow.

Play is the child's language for the expression of unconscious needs and feelings.

• These children have vivid imaginations, but in their play one detects a basis of reality. A child may take the role of policeman in play, but what he does relates to his knowledge of policeman activity. If he is Superman, what he does is a result of ideas from television. Imagination and impersonation make up a large part of their play. Imaginary playmates may be added to their play.

- They are often interested in collecting things.
- They like to be creative and express their own ideas, especially through music, art media, blocks, and role-playing.

Sense of responsibility.—As fours and fives grow more independent and secure, they grow in responsibility.

- The fours can make some wise choices and decisions.
- Fours and fives can solve many of their own problems.
- They accept and perform a few tasks at home, church, or school (within their ability and endurance).
- Fives, particularly, are dependable (within the realm of their ability), cherishing their independence.
- They can do many things for themselves.
- They are developing self-confidence and inner control.

Spiritual development.—Areas of growth are clearly seen as fours and fives learn to reason more:

- They are capable of talking to God briefly in their own words.
- They are growing in their understanding of meaning and application of Bible thoughts and stories.
- They are acquiring basic attitudes about God, Jesus, the Bible, and church.
- Fives, especially, are developing simple dependence on God (providing a sufficient sense of trust has been achieved).
- They are learning to respond positively to people and things at church.
- They may experience moments of awe and wonder and perhaps worship.

Noticeable differences in fours and fives:

- Fives generally have better emotional control. They do not cry or get angry as readily as do fours.
- Four-year-olds brag about themselves. They are bossy. They do not recognize limitations and often get into trouble. Fives are more calm, self-assured, and self-controlled.
- Fours have little feeling of group responsibility and may pursue their own interests part of the time when in a small group. Fives are more ready and interested in group participation. They enjoy the opportunity to share ideas and experiences with others.

Robert L. Jackson

• Many four-year-olds are not eager to please others. They have only vague concepts of, or interest in, fair play. Fives are interested in pleasing others—they want approval and affection from adult friends and from peers. They are willing to take turns, share, and make compromises to gain acceptance with peers.

• Fours have a fairly short attention span. They move frequently from one activity to another. The attention span of fives has increased. A child may remain at his chosen activity for a long time. He usually does not maintain such prolonged interest in a teacher-initiated activity.

• A four-year-old's question may be only temporary curiosity. He may not wait for an answer. The five-year-old wants his question answered. He may give grave consideration to the answer if it is an important matter with him. In fact, he may come back with more questions on the same subject.

• Fours have little concept of property rights. A child may use force to get what he wants. Fives have more concern for rights and feelings of others.

• Fives have more control of smaller and larger muscles.

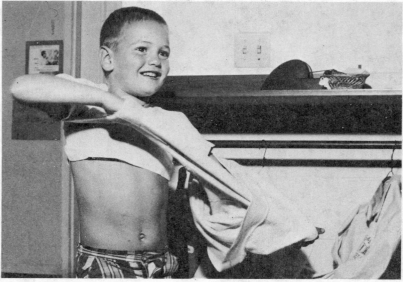

Robert L. Jackson

SIX-YEAR-OLDS (UP TO FIRST GRADE)

Some children who are six years old are still in Preschool departments at church because of the school grading system where they reside. The following are a few characteristics that may be typical of the six-year-old in the church department:

• Ready for new experiences. Reaches out for new companions, new interests, and new adults to imitate.

• Still very active. Likes to rush about. Is continually wiggling. His whole body takes part in what he does. When he writes, he has facial movements and wiggles around in his chair.

• Learns better if he has a chance to handle materials and talk about them.

• Likes to cut, paste, paint, experiment with tools and equipment.

• Needs large-muscle activities. Has problems with using pencils and materials (like needle and thread).

• Requires plenty of exercise, like building with large blocks, running, jumping, climbing, pulling, and pushing.

• Needs frequent rest periods.

- Interested in the here and now. Talks about policemen, fires, storms, animals.
- Shows different interests in play according to sex.
- Likes to be given responsibility.
- Quick to detect unfairness.

STEPS IN DEVELOPMENTAL TASKS [12]

Threes, Fours, and Fives — **Sense of Initiative**
"I have an idea!"
(*continuing a sense of trust and a sense of independence, and developing new ideas on his own*)

Toddlers and Twos — **Sense of Autonomy** (*independence*)
"Who am I, *really?*"
"I can do it myself"
(*continuing a sense of trust, and growing in independence*)

First Year — **Sense of Trust** (*through which faith is developed*)
"I need you."
"I need loving care."
"I like you."
"You like me."

The developmental tasks through the life span are developed by Erik H. Erikson.

THE OBJECTIVES OF LOVE

The developmental tasks of preschoolers are called the objectives of love by Reuel Howe. These objectives are achieved through a relationship, an interchange between child and parent and child and teachers. Through this acceptance of one another, love has the power to free each child for developing his highest potential.

To consider all that a child has to learn in the first five years, staggers one's imagination. But even more difficult than all his tasks in physical achievement are the three major tasks that influence his most important goal—the achievement of *selfhood*. These tasks are referred to as "developmental tasks."

1. *Sense of Trust* (foundation laid in the first year of life).
2. *Sense of Autonomy* (awareness of task begins in toddler age up to around three years).
3. *Sense of Initiative* (predominant in three- to five-year-olds).

SENSE OF TRUST

The baby needs a sense of trust. Will he find it?

A sense of trust is basic, and the crucial time for laying the foundations for it is during the first year of life. Trust is not fully developed at any point in childhood but may continue to grow through all of life.

Whether the baby develops trust—or mistrust—is dependent upon his environment, and particularly upon a mother figure. A loving mother (or a mother-substitute) is essential to a baby's finding trust through the comfort and love and care he receives.

The infant comes into the world that should be a safe, friendly, satisfying place for him. He is helpless and needs tender, loving care. At first, his response is to stimuli from within —hunger, thirst, pain, discomfort. A mother satisfies the baby's needs as she feeds him, holds and comforts him.

After a while, the child begins to be aware of the person caring for his needs, helping him feel safe and satisfied. He senses the gentleness of this person through the touch of her hand or the tone of her voice. This sense of trust grows as the child feels he is loved and wanted. He begins to trust others who are friendly and kind.

SENSE OF AUTONOMY (INDEPENDENCE)

Without a sense of trust, the child will not feel free to strive for a sense of autonomy or independence.

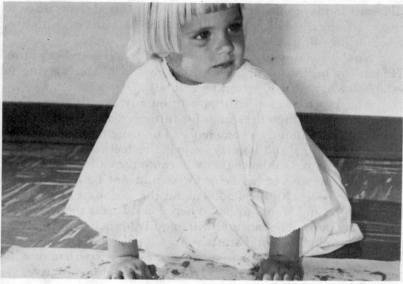

James Cooper

This search for independence may begin before the end of the first year and extend into the third year. The preschooler's tasks are not "finished products" as he passes from one to another, but one remains predominant over a period of time.

The sense of autonomy is the child's search for himself, a search for independence—the discovery of "What I can do" and "Who am I, really?" He is looking for whatever makes him feel big and strong. Over and over the one- and two-year-old must experience obstacles and taboos. Disappointments and failures are inevitable and necessary for a child's growth. This young child needs firmness and tolerance from his parents or others responsible for him. He needs sensible limitations placed on him. In this way a young child develops a sense of achievement and mastery for an all-out search for independence. If he is belittled or shamed, his growth in independence is hampered.

SENSE OF INITIATIVE

By around three, the child begins to look for new and

different kinds of satisfactions. During the period from three to five years, the child's big task is to develop his sense of initiative, a beginning of ideas.

Now, he wants to express his power to plan and organize. He has the beginning of an idea, *his own idea*. He is trying to establish what kind of person he will be.

The experiences of trust and autonomy, if satisfying to the child, will strengthen his search for initiative. During this time, the child is developing a conscience. The sense of guilt is strong in his experience, and he may be made to feel *too* guilty about too many things. Guidance that will cause the child to think less of himself because of his behavior should *not* be used. Adults need to help the child feel good about the various aspects of the person he is and wants to be. When a child feels that he is accepted as a person, he can, and will, modify his behavior to please those whom he loves and trusts.

Role-playing, imaginative play, creative experiences with various materials all help the child in his search for initiative.

CHARACTERISTIC EMOTIONAL BEHAVIOR

Each emotion is dependent upon a child's preceding emotions. As a child grows, his emotions increase in number and variety. Each step in emotional growth adds to a child's maturity. Because each child is unique, his emotional behavior will vary from that of every other child.

The following general outline showing emotional development (with regularity of patterning) is credited to Katherine Bridges:[13]

Birth:	Excitement
3 months:	Delight, excitement, distress
6 months:	Delight, excitement, distress, anger, disgust, fear
12 months:	Affection, elation, delight, excitement, distress, anger, disgust, fear
18 months:	Affection for children, affection for adults, elation, delight, excitement, distress, anger, disgust, fear

24 months:	Affection for children, affection for adults, elation, joy, delight, excitement, jealousy, distress, anger, disgust, fear
5 years:	Affection for children, affection for adults, elation, joy, delight, hope, excitement, jealousy, distress, envy, anger, disappointment, disgust, fear, anxiety, shame

6. HOW DOES THE PRESCHOOLER LEARN?

Does a child learn? The answer is *yes.* He is always learning. His learning may be positive or negative, depending on the situation and the guidance he is given. At church and home, children may be allowed to climb on tables, stand on chairs, or walk on books and pictures without guidance toward acceptable behavior. Unfortunately for the child, such experiences are poor learning situations.

WHAT IS LEARNING?

Learning is the process of changing. Some changes involved in learning are:

- Absorbing within oneself feelings, attitudes, and concepts.
- Living with others.
- Developing skills.
- Remembering previous experiences.
- Acquiring knowledge.
- Assimilating and using ideas.

SOME PRINCIPLES OF LEARNING

An individual must be ready for learning—in attitudes, experience, and knowledge.

1. Limits of learning are set by the stage of maturity of the child. (At what age should a child be encouraged to put on his own shoes? Of course there is no "pat" answer, because the whole learning process depends on each child's maturation readiness.)

2. What he learns must be based on what he already knows.

3. A child's learning is closely related to physical condition, emotions, and mental state.

4. A child's intensity of interest motivates learning.
5. A person learns gradually, as his rate of growth permits.
6. Environment affects learning.

Learning does not take place in the mind alone. The total environment in which a person learns influences learning. The climate for learning is more important than methods or tools, particularly for preschoolers. If a child feels repressed or rejected through relationships of indifferent teachers, a dismal environment, or an unpleasant atmosphere, the opportunity to learn may be rejected!

There is a difference between learning facts and learning to think.

AVENUES OF LEARNING

One's learning experience may be the result of a combination of avenues for learning. The following are some of the ways preschoolers learn:

- Through relationships with adults, the child acquires feelings and attitudes, concepts, facts, and information.
- Through the senses, a child learns to see, hear, touch, smell, and taste.
- By imitating, a child learns to do what he sees and hears others do.
- Through curiosity, a child discovers people and the world around him.
- Through repetition, a child develops skills and refinement of skills.
- By doing, a child learns independence.
- Through play, a child learns to interpret how he feels and thinks about himself and others around him; also discovers the world around him.
- Through satisfaction; a preschooler becomes discouraged if he meets too many failures. There must be plenty of time to manipulate materials, experiment with them, and develop faith in his ability to do things.

Through Relationships with Adults

Perhaps one of the greatest handicaps in understanding the learning processes of preschoolers is the adult's inability to relate learning to anything other than acquiring facts and developing skills. Yet, a teacher at church may be shocked when Tommy, a five-year-old, declares, "I don't like Mexicans." Where did he get the attitude? He did not have it at birth. He learned it through the attitude of someone in his environment.

What *do* preschoolers learn from adults? Feelings and attitudes. These are caught by the young child—one does not have to say a word! In fact, one of the best ways we teach is through unspoken communication. The younger the child, the more adults communicate without words. It is the touch of the hand, the friendly glance, the smile, and the warmth of personality that speak forcefully to the child.

James Cooper

The child senses how a parent or teacher feels about him, others, God, Jesus, the Bible, and the church through the adult's attitude more than by what he says. Debbie, a four-year-old, catches the teacher's attitude about the Bible by the way it is handled, the tone of his voice, and the expression on his face as the Bible is used. Ralph may reject the learning to "be kind" (Eph. 4:32) if the attitudes of parents or teachers do not reflect kindness toward him and others.

A child learns through grasping concepts and ideas. A child asks, "How can God see so many people at once?" Where do children get their ideas about God, Jesus, heaven, death, the world, church, the Bible—or just about anything?

Basically, a child forms his own concepts—but he develops his ideas through what he hears and sees through attitudes of others. Though a child alters his concepts as his understanding is broadened, his beginning ideas have strong impact on his thinking. At church, Phillip's teacher says: "God loves you. God loves all the people all the time." Later Phillip hears another adult say, "God doesn't like bad boys." Such experiences are confusing to him. His ideas become hazy. He may wonder: What is God *really* like? Does he like me when I hit Baby Sister?

What is a missionary? Is he someone who goes to faraway places to tell others about Jesus? Can we get this kind of concept **across to fives? Or, is it more worthwhile for a five-year-old to** relate as Tim did? When his teacher had finished telling the story of how Paul and Silas helped the people where they were in prison, Tim said, "I'm sort of a little missionary." Tim was able to express his idea of a missionary.

Feelings are more important than facts and especially for preschoolers. Do not feel that you have to always be talking to preschoolers. Sometimes you help them more by just being there. Parents and teachers need to realize that using words is not the only way to communicate the Bible message. It is also communicated by what a person does.

Sometimes the best learning is taking place when others are unaware of it.

But preschoolers *do* learn facts; they need to learn facts that will be useful to them especially at the present time. A toddler is helped to become more aware of his world by naming the objects in his environment. He sees an apple, feels it, tastes it.

Fours and fives watch apples being cut up to make a pie, or eat applesauce, or drink apple juice.

Remembering is important to learning, and a preschooler has to hear facts many times to remember them. The facts must be based on what he knows and has experienced. Too many facts, too fast, only confuse a child's learning.

The preschooler gains a lot of information through asking questions and getting answers. It is important to answer a child's question accurately and simply. Usually, he does not need or want more information than he has asked for.

James Cooper

Through the Senses

The earliest and most basic avenues of learning are through the five senses—touching, hearing, seeing, tasting, and smelling. This means that preschoolers must be encouraged to use their senses as they explore, investigate, and experiment.

For the newborn, *touching* is his way of life. In a few weeks, his perception of hearing awakens. The tone and inflection of his mother's voice impart feelings. Does the voice speak love and patience—or maybe impatience? It may be many weeks before the perception of seeing brings about the recognition of the special one caring for the infant. Then the child begins to distinguish Mother from people in general.

A child learns much through *hearing*. Some noises which are sudden and loud are frightening to a young child until he learns something about the source—a barking dog, a vacuum cleaner, trains, airplanes. As a child increases in knowledge about sources of sounds, he enjoys a simple game at home or church. Mother and child may listen for sounds and try to identify the kind of sound. Listening to music helps a child enjoy rhythmic sounds.

Experiences in *tasting* start at birth with the taste of milk, later orange juice, then cereal and egg. The growing child *works* on different textures and tastes. Some food he likes; others he dislikes; some he learns to accept after repeated offers. If the food is too sweet, too sour, too cold, or too hot, the child will be longer in accepting it.

A preschooler learns through *smell*. Recent studies indicate that the smell of food (egg, milk, meat) is directly associated with likes and dislikes in food. A child soon learns the smell of various foods and household products.

It is interesting to older preschoolers to close their eyes and think about the things they could not do if they were blind. *Seeing* helps a child learn to feed himself. As he develops motor skills and has reasonable control in getting food to his mouth, he knows how to feed himself because he has watched others eating. Seeing is important in the development of many skills as well as in the host of other learning gained through sight. Usually seeing means touching.

By Imitating

A preschooler learns much more than skills by imitating! He imitates words and deeds of those he hears and sees. As a child observes the common courtesies of everyday living demonstrated by others, he begins to incorporate them into his experience. It is good to say thank you *for* the toddler, as an example. As he catches the meaning, he will imitate the example set by a thoughtful adult.

The very young child has little feeling for the rights of

others. A child develops a feeling for others by seeing adults apply justice to him and others.

Adults are the child's example in language development. Correct words should be used in speaking so that a child will learn to speak correctly. It is good to talk to an infant. He enjoys the conversation of a friendly adult. A child learning to talk does not need to hear "baby talk" from adults.

Through Curiosity

The child wants to know! He explores, examines, takes apart, manipulates, and uses all his senses to learn what he can about his environment.

The child really lets you know how he feels.

He may ask questions when he wonders and wants to understand. The questions are not always easy. A five-year-old asked his mother: "How did the first people learn to talk? What language did they speak?" Others have asked: "Does God love children who aren't sick as much as those who are sick?" "Who helped people before Jesus was born?" "How does the world hold on?"

Adults need to answer children's questions wisely. The following principles are guides:

- Be truthful.
- Use simplicity.
- Recognize the importance of the question.
- Be accurate about information (may necessitate delay in giving an answer).
- Consider the child's reason for asking.
- Give the question immediate attention.
- Avoid gruesome or lengthy details.
- Answer in a spirit of faith.

Through Repetition

Learning is remembering. Remembering has to be developed. A preschooler may need to touch a hot radiator several times, even though the result is pain, before he learns that the experience is unpleasant.

Why does a child ask to hear the same story, the same song, the same recording, or the same book time and time again? He enjoys the repetition. This is one of his ways of learning.

By Doing

Talking is *doing*. Dressing himself, feeding himself, putting toys away are "doing" experiences for a child.

When a child indicates an interest in putting on his coat, he needs to try it. He will need help and it will take longer, but he needs the practice. Do not do for the child what he can do for himself! Skills are learned through practice.

Keep these suggestions in mind:

- Give a child only the help he needs.
- Let him take responsibility for simple mishaps, like wiping up water he spills accidentally.
- Give encouragement and praise for his accomplishments.

Other interesting and profitable doing-learning experiences are:

1. Looking at books.
2. Exploring and experimenting with science and nature (sand, water, mud, snow).
3. Caring for pets.
4. Caring for plants.
5. Participating in informal musical experiences.
6. Excursions to a farm, zoo, fire station, dairy, or other public places.

Through Play

Play is the important business of early childhood. Play is "doing." It is a child's natural way of learning.

Play is a child's best means for establishing social relationships with peers. Through play a child learns to choose favorite playmates. He learns to laugh with some children, to stay away from others.

In play, a child can deal with his fears, frustrations, or anxieties. As a child role-plays being a doctor, he may overcome a degree of fear about going to the doctor. A little girl can be the one "doing the spanking" when she plays with a doll.

Through play, children practice skills, experiment, discover, imagine, create, solve problems, and express themselves.

Play is a way of stretching the imagination.

Through Satisfaction

Although a child encounters many failures, he also has many achievements that help to balance the failures. There must be plenty of time to manipulate materials, experiment with them, and develop faith in his ability to do things.

"I can't draw a dog. Draw it for me," is a fairly good sign that an adult has helped a child feel inadequate. Perhaps an adult can say, "You draw a dog the way you like." If an adult draws or makes finished products before a child, the child may feel he cannot achieve a product acceptable to an adult or himself.

Sometimes a simple question is all that is needed for a child to feel satisfied. In block building, if a construction keeps falling, an adult may say, "Have you tried a larger block at the bottom?"

Satisfaction comes through making choices and having freedom to choose his activities. But an adult must sense when a child needs help in trying out new media. And children need experiences with many types of materials to grow in their feelings of accomplishments.

7. WHAT DOES THE PRESCHOOLER LEARN AT CHURCH?

Do children learn differently at church than they do elsewhere? Well, no, but there are developmental tasks of religious significance that children do need to learn. Perhaps some can be learned at church and others at home. For example, it is difficult to learn about the church unless a child experiences a church. There may be greater opportunities to learn about the natural world at home or with a family than within the four walls of his room at church.

"The kind of religion to which a growing person may be

able to respond is conditioned by the early emotional tone to which he [a child] is exposed," says Thelma Arnote. "Long before a child knows the words spoken to him he understands the language of feelings. He absorbs with amazing intuition and accuracy the overtones of the setting of which he is a part. If he feels love and trustworthiness in human relationships, he brings these meanings to a later conscious religious commitment. If there is miserliness and pessimism in his early emotional experience, he also brings these life experiences into his religious thinking and feeling of later years. Early experiences with the positive human emotions of love and trust may make for more eager commitment to God at a later time. The emotions of hate and mistrust may likewise make later conscious commitment to God more difficult."[14]

Teachers at church may ask and answer these questions to determine how preschoolers learn at church:

> Where does the child-person seem to be in development?
> What is his big task now?
> How does he propose to perform it?
> What problems does his striving bring to himself and others?
> How can interested adult persons help him achieve his purposes and enrich his experience?
> Is there any aspect of his present development which has significance for religious teaching? What religious experiences (if any) might be expected at this level of development? How do these come about?
> What is "teaching and learning" at this level?
> What is the ministry of a church to a child at this level?[15]

Teachers at church take on the parent role with preschoolers. Each child needs affection and concern comparable to that of loving parents. Christian faith has meaning for a child through relationship with persons who know and reflect God's love. The child needs nurture through loving, Christian friends who depend on God.

Much of the learning for preschoolers will center around teacher-child relationships and firsthand experiences. There should be much unspoken teaching, supplemented by the necessary verbal guidance.

All preschoolers should have an environment in which there are many provisions for learning and improving skills as they handle materials and deal with beginning ideas. Their social relationships will continue to be strengthened as they grow in ability to understand the joys and rights of others.

A preschooler is ready to respond to some planned teaching, but largely on an individual basis during the first years. As he matures, he is able to associate words and ideas he hears with experiences he has had, thus forming new ideas. A child's concepts about God, Jesus, the natural world, the Bible, church, home, self, others, and music can be enlarged and strengthened through books, stories, pictures, conversation, music materials, nature materials, and other firsthand experiences.

The basic needs of preschoolers at church are listed. These needs will be incorporated in each of the preschool teaching materials for preschool teachers. The degree to which the need is met varies according to the age and stage of the child.

BASIC SPIRITUAL NEEDS OF PRESCHOOLERS AT CHURCH

God: To grow in his feelings and understanding of God and what God does for people

Jesus: To have a growing understanding of Jesus

Natural world: To grow in his understanding of the natural world and his relationship to it

Bible: To become increasingly aware that the Bible tells about God and Jesus

Church: **To feel he is a part of and can participate in the fellowship of the church**

Family (Home): To grow in understanding of his place in family living

Others: To relate to persons in satisfying ways

Self: To grow in understanding of self

A child learns that teachers are willing to share some of the beginning concepts of God, Jesus, the natural world, the church, Bible, family (home), others, and himself. A child learns that he is important to teachers, the importance of other children, and the church's interest in him.

**You—the teacher, the parent—make the difference!
How much are you willing to give?**

Creative growth takes place best in a friendly environment.

The Wish

Each birthday wish
I've ever made
Really does come true.
Each year I wish
I'd grow some more
And every year
I
DO![16]

---

1. Eda J. LeShan, *The Conspiracy Against Childhood* (New York: Atheneum Publishers, 1967) , p. 326.
2. Stella Chess, Alexander Thomas, and Herbert G. Birch, *Your Child Is a Person* (New York: Parallax Publishing Co., Inc., 1965) , p. vii.
3. Mollie S. and Russell C. Smart, *Children Development and Relationships* (New York: The Macmillan Company, 1967) , p. 118.
4. *Ibid.*, p. 207.
5. James L. Hymes, Jr., *The Child Under Six* (Englewood Cliffs, New Jersey: Prentice-Hall, Inc., 1967), p. 7.
6. James L. Hymes, Jr., *Understanding Your Child* (Englewood Cliffs, New Jersey: Prentice-Hall, Inc., 1952) , pp. 4–6.
7. David Goodman, *A Parents' Guide to the Emotional Needs of Children* (Rev. Ed., New York: Hawthorn Books, Inc., 1969) , pp. 9–10.
8. *Ibid.*, pp. 26–27.
9. Reuel Howe, *Herein Is Love* (Valley Forge: Judson Press, 1961), p. 67.
10. Hymes, *The Child Under Six*, p. 95.
11. LeShan, *op. cit.*, p. 59.
12. Erik H. Erikson, *Childhood and Society* (Rev. Ed., New York: W. W. Norton and Company, Inc., 1963), pp. 247–58.
13. Horace B. English, *Dynamics of Child Development* (New York: Holt, Rinehart and Winston, 1961), p. 114.
14. Thelma Arnote, *Understanding Nursery Children* (Nashville: Convention Press, 1963) , pp. 7–8.
15. *Ibid.*, p. 8.
16. From *Child Life*, copyright 1955.

Contents to Part II

Part II

The Preschooler in Today's World

Pine Lake Farm

1. THE CENTURY OF THE CHILD

The twentieth century has been referred to as "The Century of the Child." It might also be called "The Century of the Atom," for our world has experienced vast advances in this century.

Before 1900, a child was "to be seen and not heard." This was not an attitude of disregard for the child, but simply because

73

he was considered something of "a little adult" to be reared in a respectable way to take his place in society when he reached adulthood.

Since the early part of 1900, children have been the subject of careful study, observation, research, and experimentation. The child has been an object of study in education, psychiatry, psychology, and medical science. There have been case studies, recorded notes, tape recordings, motion pictures, tests, (mental and informational), creative ability studies, and extensive studies in physical growth in an effort to learn more about child development. The results of all these endeavors have alerted parents, teachers, and specialists to new understanding and approaches in child development and rearing.

People who appear quite different may be much alike in what they do, feel, say, or think.

A DIFFERENT SOCIETY

The child today lives in a society that is different from the one in which his parents and teachers grew up. Today people are living in the greatest material prosperity our nation has known. Overabundance has changed the world for many children. Children are bored with an abundance of "things" but have not developed the ingenuity and imagination to entertain themselves.

At the extreme, the neglected and rejected child—the unloved one—has been neglected. He wanders about without adequate food, clothing, shelter, or the concern of anyone who really cares. Socially starved and intellectually stunted, he faces today's world with little hope of developing any self-esteem.

Society is in a hurry. Family tensions run high in the modern American family. Fathers work miles away from their homes at jobs children do not understand.

We live in a push-button age. Opportunities to share home chores are limited because of modern gadgets and utilities. Parents must exercise careful thought and planning for children to develop a sense of responsibility, effective habits, and desirable attitudes toward work.

IT'S HAPPENING TODAY!!!

Miracle drugs!

Computers! The push-button generation!

MICROSCOPIC WORLD!

Blood banks!

Man has seen the earth
from outer space!

ATOMIC AGE-

Apollo 10-Moon-Orbiting
Mission Successful!

Population explosion!

ASTRONAUTS
land on the moon!

Heart Transplants

DANGER!
CIGARETTE-SMOKING-

Eye Transplant!

THE SPACE AGE

Many preschoolers of today have witnessed exciting flights into space, an exploration of the moon on television. How much of this the young child can comprehend is a question, but he has caught the excitement of the experiences.

NASA

THE RACE AGE

The former concept of human dignity will have to be revised to one that embraces all human beings. Today's child hears a great deal about race riots, equal rights for all people, and integration. In school and in other associations, the child is related to ethnic groups. Perhaps it will not be difficult for young children to embrace the idea and feeling of one world of children.

PROBLEMS IN TODAY'S WORLD

Preschoolers may not understand, but they are affected by:

violence   **demonstrations**   **vandalism**
overcrowded schools   **juvenile delinquency**

immorality   race riots   war   drug addicts
    smog   divorce   overcrowded cities   child abuse

The following statements give insight into the burden which some people are feeling about today's society:

▶ Morale in American schools is at its lowest.
▶ Today's parents are lacking in spiritual qualities necessary to good emotional health for them and their children.
▶ Our government declares that a major cause for child crime is the character of parents.
▶ In overcrowded towns and cities, preschoolers have no place to play.

Surveys in high schools and colleges of America indicate that many students feel cheating, lying, and other deviations of honesty are not wrong.

There is an air of lawlessness on the part of many adults, such as taking bribes and cheating on income tax.

Though a preschooler does not understand much about these problems, he is emotionally affected. A preschooler hears and sees on television news reports that emphasize the difficulties of today. The pictures, the tone of voices, the feeling tone of announcers give to the child a sense of unrest and anxiety. He hears much on radio and in adult conversation. He sees disturbing pictures in newspapers and magazines. What lasting impressions and effects will these difficulties leave in the experience of a preschooler?

ADVANCES AND ADVANTAGES IN TODAY'S WORLD

Within the last few years and in the life span of today's preschooler, tremendous advances have been accomplished that affect him now or will in the years ahead.

space exploration   atomic age   miracle drugs
  heart and kidney transplants   automation   prosperity
    warnings about danger of cigarette-smoking
     computers   weather satellites   child study

WHAT IS COMING?

City on top of City

People with other people's hearts.

Airplanes flying 2400 miles an hour—

Need a vacation? How about— A Trip to the Moon? Contact your Outer Space Agency today!

You mean we choose the sex of our child?

24-hour work-week

Leisure Time! what to do with it?

Food! Food! Will there be enough?

Which will be the next Vietnam?

Six-Billion People by year 2000?

Many advances in the world today give the preschooler a broader range of experiences than ever before:

▶ Television (with its values and disadvantages) has afforded the child broader knowledge and understanding.
▶ Many parents are giving more attention to broadening experiences for the child through excursions (zoos, parks, museums).
▶ Appropriate educational materials, such as books, record players and recordings, wooden puzzles, and art materials are being provided.
▶ A child uses the telephone at an earlier age.
▶ More children are enrolled in nursery schools, kindergartens, day care centers, Head Start and Home Start programs.
▶ Handicapped children have opportunities for special training for development toward adjustment to living.
▶ Preschoolers are receiving learning experiences in worthwhile church programs planned to meet their needs.
▶ Increased association with ethnic groups in schools, churches, and playgrounds enlarges a child's understanding of people.
▶ More trips are being taken by auto and airplane with the family.
▶ Families are moving to new locations more often than before.
▶ Space exploration makes a child more of a world citizen than his parents.

IMPORTANT HAPPENINGS TODAY

There is much study and action toward reducing cigarette-smoking because of dangers of cancer.

• A few teen-agers are saying, "Everybody smokes pot," but warnings are out to alert youth against the dangers of drugs.

• The Apollo 8 flight to the moon was a product of centuries of scientific research and experimentation. The 400,000 engineers involved was the greatest task force ever assembled for a peaceful purpose.

On July 20, 1969, man landed on the moon. First, Neil Armstrong and then Edwin Aldrin descended their lunar module's nine-rung ladder to the surface of the moon. Television coverage made the adventure a reality for the people of the world. The adventure was considered equal to the voyage of Columbus by many people; by others, it was the most daring adventure this world has ever known.

You may never make it to the moon, but some of the preschoolers you know probably will make the trip.

• A United States astronaut has left the space program to become president of a firm that leases industrial equipment worldwide. In his job, he hopes to help develop a space station to be parked in orbit around 1975. He views this as a way to explore the earth in seeking out its mineral deposits and other natural resources.

• Many youth today are strongly motivated to be of service to mankind. This is evidenced by the large numbers who have joined Peace Corps, VISTA, the teaching profession, the Foreign Mission Board's journeyman program, the Home Mission Board's US-21 program, and other social services. They do not seem to be striving for profit and security.

• Many handicapped children face tomorrow with hope. Major strides have been made in providing educational facilities with special and individual training for overcoming handicaps.

• Advances in medical science have reached out in many directions. The lives of many preschoolers have been saved through the use of miracle drugs. Heart, kidney, and eye transplants have been successful. Blood banks have been the source of saving many lives.

• Science and technology have given us many benefits, but with advance have come new problems; for example, increased automobile accidents and polluted air and water.

Teachers and parents of preschoolers need to take into account the advantages of preschoolers today in order to guide them effectively.

WHAT ABOUT TOMORROW???

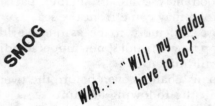

VIOLENCE...
"I don't like people being hurt."

LSD

Hippie Generation

HUNGER–
"Why does God let people be hungry?"

RIOTS!
"I'm frightened! My daddy is a policeman."

SMOG

WAR... "Will my daddy have to go?"

Automation is de-humanizing–
"What can I do?"

STUDENT REBELLION!

DRUG ADDICTS

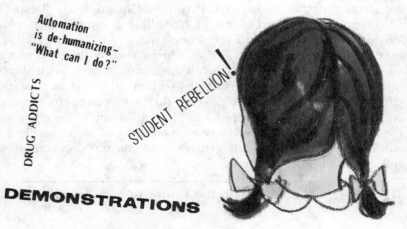

DEMONSTRATIONS

With all the advances and internal problems that exist today, we look to the future with a hope that modern man will be able to use the progress, and the problems, to make a better world through the centuries ahead.

LOOKING TOWARD THE TWENTY-FIRST CENTURY

Some estimate a world population of six billion by the year 2000. Where will all the people live? Much territory, once farmland, is already being taken to build homes, expressways, and buildings. In time, there may be city on top of city.

- Man's workweek will be reduced to as little as twenty-four hours, but he will spend many hours in study.
- In the future, a man may change occupations much more rapidly with continued advances in automation.
- Will there be enough food? Science has made rapid progress in improving crops so that greater quantities can be cultivated on less land. Such progress will have to continue if the world's people are fed. Food may come in smaller packages through processing. More food may come from the sea.
- Races will tend more and more to be as one world as people are guided to develop new attitudes, new understanding, and new wills in respect to all humanity.
- Education will see many changes even before the twenty-first century, as evidenced in the following accounts.

Some educators of today expect the school of the future to be a drastically changed institution. Children will be profiled by computers and educated according to individual needs. Within the next decade the city school, particularly in the ghetto, may no longer be a four-walled building with children coming on set schedule. There may be an education center, with flexibility to deal with the individual. An educator will work with the child and his parents to develop the proper program for the child's needs. Some children may be in school from eight to twelve hours a day. There is a need for allocating more money to education of inner-city children to overcome the disadvantages the ghetto child has suffered.

Today we have to look to the future to even be up-to-date!

2. GROUP-LIVING EXPERIENCES

TODAY'S ADULTS AND PRESCHOOLERS

Many parents feel the compulsion to speed up the growth of their preschoolers. Why should they be in such a hurry? Parents are being bombarded with such slogans as: "Don't waste these precious years!" "Teach your two-year-old to read." "Raise your child's IQ." "Start formal education early!" "Start piano lessons early."

In the last few years, with increasing pressures for academic acceleration at every level, more kindergartens, nursery schools, day care centers, and play schools are becoming available each year. The scientific and technological revolution has contributed greatly to this pressure. There is a growing fear that people in the United States may not be able to keep up with other peoples of the world.

Will rigid, formal training in early years make children smarter? Will it help them be happier, more mature socially and emotionally? Will it encourage an eagerness to learn?

Perhaps television has influenced adults' concepts about children's learning. The child who is a constant viewer amazes adults with his ability to mimic the jingles and recall the facts which he catches in advertising. Don't forget that industry knows how to appeal to the child! The child is one of the greatest consumers in today's world.

There is pressure toward formal training in memorization and accumulation of facts and information. Preschoolers may learn to imitate and memorize, but this is only one facet of learning. Learning is not just a narrow range of experiences that involve the absorption of facts and development of skills.

If a child is pushed to learn before he is ready (physically and mentally), he may get a sense of failure that will spread to tasks he has not attempted.

Many specialists in early childhood education are of the opinion that formal programs of learning will not improve a child's development—in fact, there is strong feeling that they will hinder. These educators realize that growth is a lifelong experience and cannot be hurried.

Many educators recognize the emotional problems that can arise in the pressure a child may undergo in attempting a skill for which he is not ready. Learning to read in the preschool years requires eye coordination that most children have not developed. "No long-term gains result from such teaching [too early reading]," says Dr. Harris, former president of International Council for the Improvement of Reading Instruction.[1]

There is increasing evidence that the IQ of a child or adult can be raised or lowered. Experts on intelligence and aptitude tests agree that a child who makes an inferior rating on IQ tests one day may score average or better on the test a few days later. IQ is not as unchangeable as was thought a half-century ago. IQ does not measure drive, leadership, character, ambition, or creative ability. "Pinning a child's future on his IQ rating, however, can be rather risky."[2]

HOME VALUES

Although home relations are the strongest influence in early childhood, a child is stimulated by social contacts outside the home. The opportunity for association with other young children is advantageous in a child's social development.

When a child has daily experiences in group-living, his values are somewhat influenced by the standards he senses in the environment.

How can parents get their values across to the preschooler? What if he hears neighbors or friends discuss ideas that seem to challenge the standards parents are striving to impart to their child? Be aware that the child learns most from parents. Through example, parents teach the value of human dignity. They need to hold dear the values that are meaningful to life and pass these values on to their children.

A CHURCH'S MINISTRY

The purpose of the church's ministry to children is to supplement in the child's development the same kind of nurture parents desire for him in his home.

For many preschoolers, the church building is the most important place to them outside their homes. It is the place they go regularly. Some preschoolers do not have any other opportunity for guided learning experiences with other preschoolers their age.

Today, more churches are recognizing the importance of planning and providing space, equipment, and leadership that will make it possible for every child to have the kind of experiences that will meet his needs. Parents are pleased when they know their preschooler will be happy and will have valuable relationships in rooms prepared especially for them.

Teaching materials are guides designed for teachers to gain a greater awareness of the abilities, needs, and limitations of the developmental level of preschool children. Suggested schedules reflect flexibility and variety. Suggestions for individual, small group, and large group activities help teachers in a variety of situations. Singing; telling Bible stories; using Bible thoughts, books, educational toys, recordings, pictures, and musical instruments are some methods used in teaching religious truths to pre-schoolers.

The basic spiritual needs for preschoolers related to the eight subject-matter areas (God, Jesus, the natural world, the Bible, church, family, others, and self) are given on page 69. Desired outcomes express what is expected of a toddler, three-year-old, four-year-old, or five-year-old in relation to each of these subject-matter areas. In the examples of desired outcomes which appear, the format in which the desired outcomes are stated reveals the progression from the baby-toddler stage on up to the four- to five-year stage. The desired outcomes at each level are closely in-terrelated. For instance, achievement of the baby-toddler out-come is basic to achievement at the two-three level, and the achievement at the two-three level is basic to achievement at the four-five level. Achievement at any level is not a once-and-for-all thing. The toddler who is familiar with the Bible increases his familiarity with it during the rest of his preschool years; in fact, we hope he will become increasingly familiar with it throughout his entire life. A child lacking exposure to the Bible in the first two years of life cannot become familiar with the Bible as a baby or toddler. But he must become familiar with it before he truly knows that it reveals God's love.

The desired outcomes stated here are only examples. Other desired outcomes in each area are dealt with in the curriculum materials.

Desired Outcomes
(stated in terms of each child)
God

Baby-Toddler:	Experiencing happy feelings asso-ciated with God
Two-Three:	Having awareness that God loves him
Four-Five:	Recognizing a dependence upon God and his love

Jesus

Baby-Toddler:	Experiencing happy feelings asso-ciated with Jesus

Robert L. Jackson

Two-Three:	Having an awareness of Jesus as a special baby
Four-Five:	Experiencing wonder and joy at the coming of Jesus

Natural World

Baby-Toddler:	Discovering the beauties and wonders around him
Two-Three:	Accepting some responsibility in taking care of things God has made
Four-Five:	Accepting increasing responsibility in caring for things which God creates

Church

Baby-Toddler:	Developing a growing sense of at-homeness in his room at church
Two-Three:	Understanding that the church building is a special meeting place where one can have satisfying experiences

Four-Five: Experiencing satisfaction in fellowship with church people

Bible

Baby-Toddler: Becoming familiar with the Bible as a book

Two-Three: Developing an awareness that the Bible contains stories about God and Jesus

Four-Five: Discovering that the Bible is important because it reveals God's love and care for all people

Family

Baby-Toddler: Associating experiences he has at home with those he has at church

Two-Three: Participating in a variety of activities at church that reveal family experiences at home

Four-Five: Relating Bible teachings about family living to personal home life

Others

Baby-Toddler: Experiencing happiness in his relationship with others

Two-Three: Accepting some responsibility for helping others

Four-Five: Developing an ability and desire to help others and to work with them

Self

Baby-Toddler: Feeling security in his environment

Two-Three: Developing a good feeling about himself and the choices he makes

Four-Five: Developing a favorable view of himself; and an awareness that each person is an individual of worth

Church experiences are not always easy for a child.—A toddler who suddenly becomes aware of the separation from his parents may cry when he is brought to his department. Toddlers and twos have had limited experiences; therefore, they must be continually reassured that their parents will return for them. A child usually goes into his room more willingly if he is allowed to walk in by himself. Sometimes adults literally push a crying child in the door. Help! Parents and teachers need a talk. Talk about how the child must feel about separation. A teacher's task is to help a child feel comfortable and secure in the room at church. Wait . . . show interest. Wait . . . a lap and a pat. Wait . . . hold the child's hand as you discover interesting materials around the room.

Fours and fives usually come into the room freely. But watch for a child who is suddenly timid or aggressive or angry. Be ready when a child needs you. Your nearby presence will help. A kind word, a smile, or a pat on the shoulder may help.

There are various occasions when preschoolers are at church (because parents have meetings) that are difficult for a number of reasons: WMU meetings, adult choir rehearsals, revival meetings, study groups, planning meetings, Wednesday night programs, and extended sessions on Sunday.

Many meetings are lengthy. When a preschooler is in Sunday School, Training Union, and Extended Session on Sundays, he may become physically tired and overly stimulated from the long period of time in a group.

The same teachers are not with the preschoolers during each session, and often a weekday teacher has little training in guiding preschoolers. This can be confusing and disturbing to a child.

Preschoolers are not always in the same familiar room. Age groups that are separated on Sunday may be combined during the week. A preschooler may be in a room in which the materials and equipment are not suitable for the kinds of experiences he needs.

New teachers! Strange room! Unfamiliar children! Disturbances at home! Illness! Teachers who threaten! What is the ministry of the church when preschoolers need help?

- An understanding teacher
- The same room each time a preschooler comes to church
- Opportunities for preschoolers to interact with other children and teachers
- A sensitive teacher who detects illness
- Opportunities for parents and teachers to discuss needs of children
- Ways to train all teachers in understanding and guiding children.

J. Carey Wood

Worship services.—A preschooler usually attends worship services with his parents around age four. Parents can help the child adjust by following some of these suggestions. Perhaps you can share some of these ideas with parents:

- Take the child to the worship service at night. This service is more informal, and parents may feel that their child is not as likely to disturb.

- If the child is restless, the parents may not want him to stay through the entire service.
- Sit where leaving will be unnoticed if leaving the service is necessary.
- Allow the child to hold a hymnbook when the congregation sings.
- Do not expect him to sit still all the time.
- Permit him to go to sleep if he needs to.
- Commend him for his behavior when he deserves it.

Moral values must be established in the home through the right example and consistent guidance by parents.

NURSERY SCHOOLS

The nursery school serves the needs of preschoolers who are usually three and four years of age, although some schools accept children at two-and-a-half years of age. The experiences offered are adapted to what is now known about the growth needs of these age levels. The nursery school teachers share with parents the responsibility for promoting sound growth in a period when growth is rapid and important.

Parents are asking:

"Shall I send my child to nursery school?"

Most educators feel that three- and four-year-olds benefit from nursery school if it is a good one.

- A child with no brothers or sisters gets special pleasure and stimulation from nursery school.
- Nursery school is a means of loosening emotional ties of parent and child.
- A wide range of activities is provided.
- A child from a rigid home may profit by the greater flexibility of nursery school.
- Nursery school is important for a slum-area child or deprived child.
- Children who live in apartment complexes and housing areas where outside play is restricted need the freedom which a nursery school provides.

Today it is almost as difficult to get children into some nursery schools as it is to enrol in college.

What does nursery school offer?

1. Opportunities for regular companionship with friends his own age in a carefully planned setting, under skilled guidance are offered. The school provides occasions for taking turns, cooperation, self-assertion, and self-defense. The experiences contribute to the child's social and emotional development.

2. The child has opportunities to improve motor development and control with challenging, appropriate equipment and with space and freedom to use the equipment.

3. The child develops his intellectual faculties through constant stimulation and mind-stretching experiences with materials that are appropriate to his skills.

How do I choose a nursery school?

Choosing the right nursery school seems as complicated as choosing the right college! Simply trying to prepare the child for some later time is not a worthy goal. The purpose should be to help the child have the best experience possible each day.

There are many unqualified and unsuitable people operating nursery schools. Do not be misled by clever names or extensive advertising.

Visit the school, or several schools, before deciding on one. Look for special features, like:

• **Teachers who are warm, responsive, relaxed, and loving,** and who are licensed by their state. (Beware of a situation in which the head teacher is one who has taught second or third grade for years.) The teacher is the key in choosing a nursery school. The building and equipment do not count for much if the teacher is ineffective. See the teacher in action. Does she appear interested in children? Do the children seem stimulated and happy?

• **The physical facilities available. Nursery schools range** from remodeled farm houses to elaborate brick structures. Some are in church basements. Is the school clean, safe, well-ventilated,

Bryce Finch

with sufficient child-size bathroom facilities?

• The outdoor and indoor equipment. Does the outdoor area provide adequate space that is safe from traffic or other hazards? Does the inside equipment and furnishings vary so that there is opportunity for free dramatic play, cooperative play, creative art, and music? Beware of a preschool with lots of tables or one from which children go home every day with something they have traced or colored within prescribed lines.

• The programed routine for the school. Are there alternate active and quiet times, large-muscle play, free activity that is individual and creative? Avoid schools that have regimentation with organized game-playing and directed musical activities.

• The regular procedure for enrolling the child. In many schools, the child has to be interviewed for acceptance.

• The requirements in a state for operating nursery schools vary. In some states, there are no mandatory requirements for nursery schools. Check with the Education Department and the Child Welfare Department in your state to see that the school meets requirements for a good program.

Some states require that only the head teacher be certified. Assistants do not have to be certified. There are states with no standards for teacher-training.

• In most good schools, the cost is high. Qualified teachers must be paid salaries equivalent to public schools in order to attract them.

There are many excellent nursery schools; others are poor. Investigate carefully before deciding on a school.

KINDERGARTENS*

The first private kindergarten in America was established in 1855, and the first public kindergarten began in 1873. Today some states provide public school kindergarten for all five-year-olds. Other states have no public kindergartens.[5]

As with nursery schools, the quality of kindergartens varies greatly. In some states, the schools have well-equipped rooms, with provision for appropriate creative activities for worthwhile learning experiences for fives (some kindergartens include fours). They have teachers with training in early childhood education. Unfortunately, most kindergartens are severely overcrowded. Whereas the top enrollment should not exceed more than twenty-five, a teacher may have thirty to fifty in a room. Of course, there is no possibility for a close teacher-child relationship when enrollments are so large.

In most public schools, there are two groups of kindergartners. One group is enrolled for a morning session, and another for afternoon. This leaves little time for teachers to work closely with parents which is so needed at this age.

Another factor that has damaged the quality of kindergarten work is America's panic over early reading. The pressure has converted many kindergarten programs to resemble those of first grade (workbooks, formal reading).

When asked, "How can we get our kindergartner ready for

Kindergartens are usually for children one year away from first grade.

first grade?" a wise educator answered, "Let him be a kinder-gartner!"

In states where kindergarten is not a part of public school, one may find private kindergartens. Often these are located in churches and compose a part of the church's total educational program. These may or may not include religious emphasis in the materials and procedures.

As with nursery schools, the quality of private kindergartens ranges from excellent to poor. The teacher may be well trained in early childhood education with assistants who have less formal training. In some cases, a teacher may not have reached training beyond that received in the training program of the church.

A church kindergarten usually is subsidized with funds from the church budget plus a tuition charge to preschoolers enrolled. This program includes a religious emphasis supplementing the church's preschool program.

Parents considering enrolling children in private kinder-gartens need to follow the same general principles suggested for choosing a nursery school.

J. Carey Wood

"Our impatience prevents the cultivation of great minds and big souls. It is almost impossible to hasten the cultivation of a good life. Assimilation of the good is a slow process." [4] "We want our five-year-olds to conduct themselves like adults . . . because it is convenient for us. . . . There is a time when everyone should behave like a five-year-old, and that is when he is five. We rob our children of their childhood when we hurry them through it at our wicked pace." [5]

Preparing for kindergarten.—If a five-year-old has not attended nursery school, entrance into kindergarten will be a giant step into the outside world. There are many ways parents can help the child take the step in confidence.

• Visit the school during the spring before the child enters in the fall semester. Most public schools plan for a child to visit in the security of his parent's presence. There is the opportunity to meet the teachers and view the room.

• Give your child materials to develop appropriate skills: large blocks for building, cutting and pasting materials, wooden inlay puzzles, large crayons and paintbrushes (brush, $\frac{3}{4}$ inch wide) and large sheets of paper to create his own pictures. Provide him books (check out from church and public library) that are attractive in format and content to stimulate his thinking.

• Lead your child to assume a few responsibilities in helping at home.

• Guide your child in good health habits—cleanliness, rest, and eating.

• Instruct your child in a few simple safety rules that will protect him when he is on his own.

• Trust your child and show confidence in him.

DAY CARE CENTERS

For a working mother who cannot care for her baby or preschool child during the day, a good day care center is a possible solution. Children are cared for by adults (some well trained; others less qualified) where the routine of meals, naptime, and play are supervised by a community organization, a local family agency, or a church.

Again, parents must choose a center with care. Some centers have a good program; others are ineffective in various ways.

An organization responsible for the regular daytime care of preschoolers should be licensed by the state. This means the organization should meet the minimum requirements for health, facilities, meals, and safety.

A day care center differs from a nursery school in its purpose —to provide safety and routine care of children whose parents are not able to care for and guide them during the day. Children usually remain in a center from about 9:00 A.M. until 5:00 P.M. A good center should fulfill its basic purpose.

Parents should check on (1) the health and physical facilities of a day care center, (2) the opportunities for a child to play with other children his age, (3) the friendliness and understanding of the staff who care for and supervise the children, and (4) parent participation.

PLAYGROUND AND PARK AREAS

Many communities work hard to provide playground and park areas where preschoolers can be taken by parents for outdoor play. Some are on school grounds.

A neighborhood park may be equipped with sturdy outdoor equipment, a sand area, and a surfaced space for riding wheeled toys.

In large complexes of apartments or other multiple housing units, there may be a play area. This is usually equipped with a few pieces of outdoor items, such as swings or slides. The equipment often is not very durable or safe. Sometimes the area is large enough for preschoolers to pull wagons or ride tricycles.

Some mothers who live in multiple housing units work out arrangements for supervising several children for a period each day, each mother taking her turn.

For children who are not enrolled in nursery school, the play areas provide a chance for social experiences with peers as well as a chance for large-muscle development.

PUBLIC NURSERY FACILITIES

These special kinds of services are normally found in large cities. In bowling alleys and other places of amusement, parents may find a nursery available for the convenience of patrons. A large shopping center sometimes arranges nursery facilities where mothers may leave young children while they shop. There is generally a small fee charged for the service.

Arrangements for public nursery service may be convenient for the parent, but is the experience a desirable one for the child? Is the room spacious and clean? Are there adequate and appropriate furnishings and play materials? Is the attendant trained in child care? What are the chances of a child catching infectious diseases?

GRANDPARENTS IN THE HOME

In many families, one grandparent, and sometimes both, is part of the family household.

Having a grandparent in the home has many values. The grandparent's room offers a good place for a preschooler to relax from the pressures of a crowded or hurried household. A grandparent usually has more time to talk, to listen, and to play. A grandparent's stories about the child's own parents when they were young help the child understand that his parents are human too! The extra affection a child receives from the grandparent reinforces the emotional well-being of the child.

When a grandparent lives in the home, a child can do a variety of chores to help him.

A grandparent in the home is in a position (unless physically or otherwise unable) to serve as a substitute for an ill, absent, or overpressured parent. A child's world is broadened when he finds that persons other than his parents can take good care of him.

Having a grandparent talk about past experiences of various members of the family helps the child in his developing concepts of family relations. The preschooler's ability to grasp relationships is vague. Perhaps Sue, five years old, did not fully understand when she shared this bit of information with her teacher at church: "It's going to be a long time before I'm a mommy. Then my mother will be changing into a grandma and my daddy to a grandpa, but he will still be my daddy!"

On occasion, there may be another relative living in a child's home for a time. Perhaps an aunt or uncle is attending college in the area where the child's family resides. The student may live in their home while in college. Whatever the relationship, it is an occasion for the child to enlarge his concepts about family ties and a time to value and accept others into the home.

HOMES WITH OLDER CHILDREN

Interaction with other children in the family affects a child's social behavior. The relations are significant in determining what the child thinks of himself, also his attitudes toward others.

There is often fear that the younger child will be pampered and spoiled, and it does occur in some cases. The oldest child may be disturbed that parents seem to place more affection on the young child, but this also would happen only in some situations.

It has been noted that the greater the age difference in children, the more likely there will exist a friendly, protective attitude rather than jealousy.

It seems to matter little to the infant during the first five or six months as to who holds him, feeds him, or changes his diaper as long as the child feels secure. In the middle of the first year, however, a radical change comes. The child becomes much aware of the person who is caring for him. A deepened dependency develops. If mothers can be with the child from eighteen months to three years, the child will not feel abandoned. Around three, children feel somewhat secure with other children their age and mother-substitutes.

If there is a child under three years of age in the home and the mother works, the most suitable plan is to have a baby-sitter who can come to the home for the day. The person needs to be:

- Someone who likes children and gets along well with them.
- A person conscientious in carrying out the mother's plans and wishes.
- Someone who can deal with emergencies.
- An understanding person who desires to meet the demands with standards that approximate the parents' standards.

If the person is already a real friend, she may have better relations with the child. It is important that the child be happy and feel secure with the mother-substitute.

It is helpful if parents know something about the life and ambitions of the one who fills this responsibility in their home.

Be sure the baby-sitter understands what is expected of her (him).

3. PRESSURES OF TODAY

Perhaps one of the most damaging influences today is the pressure put on children, as well as on other family members,

Robert L. Jackson

due to the rapid pace of life in general. There seems to be little time for relaxed family life when each one can enjoy the other. With commuting fathers and working mothers, there is constant demand to meet one schedule or another.

Some parents put everything important on a strict schedule —eating, sleeping, and a child's daily hurried routine—in order to do things that are really less important. In a desperate attempt to force the child (who is not in a hurry) to meet adult schedules, conflicts in parent-child relationships are built.

"The adult who rules by clock instead of by common sense will produce tension . . . in his children. . . . The removal of unnecessary time pressures will do more to diminish friction between parents and children than any 'design for discipline' we can evolve." [6]

Pressure of time applies to anyone who guides children. In church procedures with preschoolers, it is easy to become so concerned about what teachers want to accomplish that individual needs are forgotten.

EFFECTS OF TELEVISION

Parents continually search for answers to questions arising about television. The more common questions are: How much television-watching should children be exposed to? How can certain programs be closed to children's looking? What programs create fears and anxieties? Will children's eyes be damaged? What should a family do when programs clash with mealtime and bedtime?

Such questions asked must be answered in different ways for different children. For a child under six, it seems highly desirable to limit both the amount of looking and listening. The preschooler needs much activity, doing things, handling materials, and exploring the world around him. There are few programs appropriate for this age. This leaves the responsibility directly on the parent or the person in whose charge parents leave their children.

Other helpful guides include: (1) See that a child does not sit too close to the screen. Make opportunities to have the viewing broken at intervals. (2) Keep the family timetable somewhat flexible to avoid clashes. Occasionally, the whole family may watch a special program. (3) Plan ahead for special programs to watch—music, drama, art, science, travel.

Values of Television

—Television has had a great impact in making the world more of a "one world." Within a few minutes it is possible to know an important news happening in any part of the world. People feel they know more about peoples and places of the world through actual happenings viewed on television.

—It is an important educational tool when properly used.

—It may expand a child's vocabulary if the right kind of programs are viewed.

—It enlarges the child's concept of many subjects.

—Television can broaden the child's reading interest

—It can be the means of uniting the family in a common interest.

Dr. Haim G. Ginott summarizes some thoughts on television:

On one fact all agree. Television consumes a significant
part of a child's day. More of his time is spent with the
TV set than with his father or mother. . . . Parents have a
right to protect their children from exposure to daily doses
of sordid sex and vivid violence. While children need not
be sheltered from all tragedy, they should be protected
from entertainment in which man's brutality to man is
not a tragedy, but a formula.[7]

RACE PROBLEMS

Preschoolers are aware of rioting and unrest among racial
groups in the society of today. They are questioning and wonder-
ing (maybe not in a verbal way). They are concerned. They are
developing attitudes.

Race attitudes are learned early in life. Many fours are
aware of racial differences. Fives talk about racial differences.

On the basis of research studies, Mary Ellen Goodman declares that prejudice may be firmly set by six or eight years.[8]

Dr. Goodman believes teachers can help weed out prejudice
in young children by:

- Giving constructive guidance when prejudice appears.
- Helping a child think of people as individuals and not
  as groups, such as religious, social, or racial.
- Discouraging the use of such labels as "Mexican," "white,"
  "black," "Negro," or "brown."

The following guidance suggestions may be useful to teachers who are responsible for working with ethnic and integrated
groups. Ways to help a child feel good about himself and to have
an optimistic look about growing up:

- Help him develop all his strength and try to meet all his
  needs, not just mental or emotional.
- Help each child feel that he is a person, lovable and capable of contributing something valuable to others.

**"A child's life is so full of restrictions, regulations, and frustra-
tions that media of release become essential. Music is one of the
best avenues of release: it gives sound to fury, shape to joy, and
relief to tension."[9]**

MOBILITY OF POPULATION

"Dad, why do we have to move away?" Giving a satisfying answer to this question, especially to a preschooler, is not easy.

Today thousands of people are moving from one part of the country to another. Some families move two or three times within a year. Some children seem to thrive on the excitement and change. Others find moving difficult and need parents to smooth the way.

In less than one hundred years, the United States has changed from an agricultural society to a city people. Hoping for better job opportunities, families have left the farm and small town for big cities. More than seventy percent of the people in the United States will soon be living in urban complexes. Cities are not prepared to cope with this sudden growth. Many are congested, have inadequate housing and transportation, and are burdened with poverty, unemployment, and welfare problems. Today's preschoolers are involved in the experience of living in crowded apartment buildings and small housing units. There is little or no outdoor area in which to play.

Parents need to make moving as easy as possible for a child.

- Start talking about the move early.
- On moving day, concentrate on helping the child feel secure and safe as he sees the belongings loaded into a moving van. Let him keep a favorite toy or blanket with him.
- Show the child his new home or a picture of it. As much as possible, explain *why* you are moving.
- Spend extra time with him on moving day; even though it is difficult to take time.
- During the actual moving, at least one parent should go on the trip to the new home.
- Be sure to pack old battered toys that are favorites of the child. They will be "security" for him in the new home.
- Help the child feel at home in the new home. Welcome into your home new friends that he finds nearby. Arrange his room much like his old one.
- Feel happy yourself about the move.

Church leaders can help the new child in the neighborhood. Invite families to church who move near you. Welcome with warmth a new child who comes to your department on Sunday.

A PRESCHOOLER NEEDS TO BE ALONE

Let it happen! Give your child a chance to be alone. In their haste in changing from one activity to another, parents overlook the child's need to be by himself at some time during the day.

A child needs what one educator has called "occupied aloneness." He needs to get to know himself. He needs time to think. A child needs to know how to spend time alone, how to do "nothing" once in a while. Many adults are actually frightened when they see a child who appears unoccupied; they think something is wrong with the child!

WORKING MOTHERS

The number of working mothers of children under six seems to be increasing yearly. Why?

Is the working mother neglecting her children? Are children of working mothers doomed to be delinquents? Why do some mothers feel guilty because they work while other working mothers feel no guilt? These questions arise often and must be answered by mothers today.

Sociologists offer this opinion: "If the working mother arranges good care for her children in her absence, they are no more likely to be delinquent than adequately supervised youngsters whose mothers do not work. . . . If the mother remains at home but does not keep track of her child, he is more likely to become a delinquent." [10]

The quality of motherhood should not be confused with quantity, it is not the twenty-four hours a day "on duty" for a mother that determines whether she is a good mother. The question is: Can a good mother who works give her child adequate nurture and love in the time she spends at home? The quality of parent-child relationship is more important than the amount of time involved.

There are still many in professional groups who feel that the mother's place is in the home. However, most of the evidence about effects on the child is in theory and not fact.

The effects on a child when a mother works differ with various preschoolers. The results depend on other factors that interact with the mother's absence:

- Age of the child
- The mother's motive for working
- The mother's competency at child-rearing
- The skill of the mother-substitute
- The father's schedule and his attitude about the mother working
- The parents' relationship with each other

Even though the mother works of necessity or by choice, she discovers that her hardest problem of management comes while the children are young. These years are of great importance to the growth and personality of the child when a mother's influence can have the most value.

It is important that the reactions of the mother-substitute

to the child and her methods be similar to those of the mother. If a younger child is enrolled in a daytime program, such needs may or may not be met.

The key to success for the working mother is that she fulfill her role as wife and mother. Interaction with Christian friends helps to supplement her understanding of her life's role.

ABSENTEE FATHERS

Some preschoolers may go for days with hardly a glimpse of the father, even when they are living in the same household. In many fields of labor, the work is divided into three shifts so that there is never a stopping place except for holidays. When a father's working hours are at night and he has to sleep part of the day, there are times when he has very little association with his children.

Today, many young couples with one or two children are arranging for the father to complete college. If he works and attends classes too, he is an "absentee" father in the home. Other absent fathers are: those who are separated from their family because of military service, men whose work requires traveling long distances from home, and the moonlighting father who takes a second job because of financial burdens.

Absence of the father puts added responsibility in child-rearing in the hands of the mother. Although married, she is almost a widow. In many cases, the mother "lives" for the children. She smothers them with excessive care and overprotection, thus dominating and hindering individual development of the children.

As with the working mother, the quality of father-child relationship during the times they are together can offset some of the difficulties of separation. A father cannot have an emotionally healthy family if he does not invest time in his wife and children. A father cannot capture the pleasurable hours he could have shared with his children. "Hello, Son. . . . Goodbye, Son," can be a passing slogan for a father. Or it can be filled with joy, laughter, tears, or love shared deeply with the family.

Churches are encouraged to have qualified men as teachers

in the Preschool department. A man teacher is a welcome father-substitute by preschoolers. This experience will aid in the security of the child who has limited associations with his own or no father.

1. Morton Edwards, *Your Child—Today* (New York: Permabooks, 1960), p. 105.
2. Ibid., pp. 156–57.
3. James L. Hymes, Jr., *The Child Under Six* (Englewood Cliffs, New Jersey: Prentice-Hall, Inc., 1967) , p. 224.
4. Harold E. Kohn, *Pathways to Understanding* (Grand Rapids: Wm. B. Eerdmans Publishing Co., 1958), p. 113.
5. Ibid., p. 113.
6. Edwards, op. cit., pp. 59–61.
7. Haim G. Ginott, *Between Parent and Child* (New York: Avon Books, 1960), pp. 140–41.
8. Morton Edwards, *Your Child from 2 to 5* (New York: Permabooks, 1955), pp. 246–47.
9. Ginott, op. cit., p. 95.
10. Edwards, *Your Child—Today,* p. 43.

Contents to Part III

Part III

Facing Today with the Preschooler

Some days *everything* seems to be wrong. Yes, even preschoolers have their problems. Today's children are not the first ones to have problems. In all times and in all circumstances, children have had problems in learning to live in the world of things and people.

In different generations, problems seem to take on new meaning, and they are often viewed in a new way. The following descriptions are indicators of problems and how they were handled in past years.

1. YESTERDAY'S PROBLEMS

Toilet training.—In the 1920's and 1930's, many experts thought that the sooner parents got started with toilet training the better. In many instances, it seemed to be a matter of rivalry among mothers. Training methods were rigid. Training was enforced in spite of natural needs.

Some pediatricians thought if parents started early enough and were firm enough, they could hope for a completely "trained" child as early as eight, twelve, twenty, or thirty-two weeks. These successes, when they occurred, were more the successes of the mother than the baby. "The infant who is trained early and remains trained is most often the good learner but one who lacks inner spontaneous growth forces." [1]

He may live to be 80 years old! Can't we give him just a few months to be a baby?

Overcoming fears.—Push the child into the situation and he will get over his fear has been a rather popular idea in the past.

David is afraid of water. Throw him in!

Mary is afraid of the dark. Send her to the basement at night by herself.

Jim falls off the packing box. Put him back up again.

Many parents followed this unfeeling policy because they believed it was the way to cure fears in a child.

Another approach to fears was to shame the child in an effort to stop the fear.

Threats that created fears were used as a means of controlling the child: "If you are not good, the bogeyman will get you." "The policeman will get you if you do that." "If you do that again, I won't love you." What kinds of feelings were left in the mind of the child?

Thumb-sucking.—Many methods were used to stop a child from sucking his thumb. Mechanical devices called thumb-guards were placed on the thumb so that the child could not get to the thumb. Bitter aloes were rubbed on the thumb and fingers to discourage the child from sucking. Shame was used commonly, and young children hid behind doors or in closets to get peace with their thumb-sucking. Such methods only added to the child's frustration and did not get to the real cause.

Heredity.—The wrong ideas that people believed about heredity ranged from superstition to lack of understanding. Several fallacies about what could be inherited were common in the past. (1) The genes inherited determine what a child will be, and nothing can be done about it. (2) A shock to the mother during pregnancy can cause her unborn child to be "marked." (3) Children can inherit communicable diseases from parents.

Sex.—Where do babies come from? Fifty years ago the subject of sex was taboo. Parents were brought up to feel that sex should be secret. This handicapped parents from feeling free to share their feelings openly. If a child asked where babies come from, he was usually told that a stork brings them. Evasive answers were often given with embarrassment. At times a parent would assure the child that when he got older, he would understand.

Retarded.—Until the end of World War I, the severely retarded child was placed in an institution where he received nothing more than custodial care or he was kept in the home —scarcely more than a "vegetable." Little or no effort was made to bring out self-confidence in his abilities.

2. RECOGNIZE PROBLEMS AND MEET SPECIAL NEEDS

A preschooler's need may be physical, emotional, or social. Behavior is the cue. Parents and teachers must look beyond the behavior to discover the source of anxiety, fear, or other emotional problems.

Children *do* have problems in growing up. It is inevitable that every child will experience unhappiness, discomfort, frustration, disappointment, tensions, fears, and anxiety. One childhood educator has referred to children's problems as "troubles." Indeed, a child who has problems is one who is troubled in some way. It is up to parents and teachers to discover what it is that troubles a child and makes his behavior objectionable to others.

Bad behavior is an indicator that something is bothering a child.

As some ideas about general behavior are known, one is able to recognize a pattern in behavior and to understand how to approach the preschooler in his need. In growth, the general trend is toward improvement in behavior, but with preschoolers it is not steady and uninterrupted. It does not go forward consistently without regressing. Each age level has its positive as well as its negative behavior.

A child seems to be in better balance at some ages; then he alternates and is unhappy and confused with himself and the world. There seems to be an alternation of stages—from better to worse, then back to better.

If a child's behavior suddenly takes a turn for the worse, the reason may not be something wrong in his environment nor that he is "bad." It may be the stage he goes through. At one year, a child may demand to feed himself. A two-and-a-half-year-old's behavior becomes demanding and self-centered. The five who feels able and stable becomes the explosive six. One kind of behavior appears to be as necessary to growth as the other.

"If we can accept all of these extremes, 'for better or for worse,' as necessary parts of growth . . . we will be looking at things realistically." [2]

Knowing that unacceptable behavior is probably just a stage will help parents and workers be a little more relaxed about the child, but it does not mean accepting the behavior without helping a child to correct it. Knowing what to expect of preschoolers may help adults cope with behavior more successfully.

Whatever a child says or does is meaningful. It reveals his personality, his needs, his strivings, and his difficulties. Many forms of behavior which often disturb parents and teachers indicate acute needs, heavy burdens, unresolved conflicts, and emotional disturbances for which the child needs parental help. Let's take a look at some of the common problems which preschoolers have.

WHO AM I? WHO ARE YOU?

The toddler is on an intensive search to find out who he is. Will the toddler find that he is a person who can discover that he is in an interesting world, and that he can depend on people? If things go well for him, he learns to feel that he is an important person, that he is one who can explore and discover, one who can create. He develops self-confidence. He is somebody! This attitude about self is a result of many experiences of being treated with respect by others from the beginning of life. By the time he is four, he has developed a good feeling about himself. If, however, he has been rejected by others, his chances of acquiring a good self-image are limited.

The two-to-four-year-old is developing a sense of others. "Who are you?" he asks, as be begins to sense himself as only one among many. He is becoming interested in, and aware of, others. He is interested in the attitudes and opinions of others. He is beginning to know something about others as he has opportunities in group relationships. As he associates with peers, he discovers what they are like and what interests they have. A love for self is basic. Jesus gave the admonition, "Love your neighbor *as yourself.*"

EATING

Most parents are anxious when their child does not eat enough. Eating is an area of development in which adults are apt to force a child beyond his needs.

A child's appetite diminishes after his first year, and he probably will not show much interest in food again until he reaches school age. The foods he likes and accepts (usually meat, fruit, milk, and bread and butter) contain every element he needs. Refusal of new foods cause parents to be concerned.

From one year to about eighteen months, two things interfere with the child's eating. Motor drive makes it difficult for him to sit long enough to eat; yet the desire to feed himself takes longer and tires him easily. Give him food that he can handle with his fingers.

Drinking from a cup may be of little interest to the young toddler. Insistence on drinking from a cup should be minimized at this stage. Around twenty-one months, a child's taste may become discriminating. He may accept only one brand of baby food; he may depend upon a certain bib, spoon, cup, or dish as part of a successful meal. Because the child does not have words to express his needs, he may cry until the parent guesses the answer.

A child's poor eating habits in the third year may be even more distressing to a parent. The child has indecisive and finicky choices. Choices may be related to taste, form, consistency, or color. He may want foods very separate—not touching each other.

During the second and third year, appetites fluctuate from

Robert L. Jackson

very good to very poor. Allow for this fluctuation within reason. If the child is allowed to pour his own milk from a small pitcher to his cup, this may motivate drinking his milk.

Appetite usually increases in the four-to-five-year period. The child's choices and acceptance of foods are wider if he is given an increasing number of foods from which to choose.

What about the bottle? Many infants give up the bottle by the end of the first year. A few cling to the bottle. Drastic changes in the nipple (color, style, or enlargement of holes) at about fifteen or eighteen months may help the child give up the bottle. Some children are so attached to the bottle that it is wise to continue a bottle at bedtime until two or possibly three years. The bottle often induces sleep and insures milk intake.

Fours and fives gain increasing control of muscles and learn to eat with forks and can even use knives. They learn to talk easily during mealtime.

General Rules to Help Children Enjoy Good Food

- Serve food attractively.
- Give small helpings.
- Serve food without comment.
- Do not stress amount of food to be eaten. Many children who have small appetites to begin with absolutely revolt at any mention of how much food they are expected to eat.

- Try to maintain a calm, unworried attitude toward the child's eating. Nothing creates a feeding problem more quickly than an overanxious attitude on the part of parents.
- Don't stress table manners with young children. Manners can come later when a positive attitude toward eating has been established.
- Allow finger feeding until the child has become fairly proficient at eating and is interested in food.
- Do not have the child eat at the family table until you find that he is ready to do so.[3]

SLEEPING

As with other areas of life, preschoolers develop patterns of sleep. Preschoolers vary greatly in the amount of sleep they get and require, in the depth of sleep, and in the ease with which they go to sleep and awaken.

There is no best way for getting a child to sleep. For an infant, rocking seems to be one of the greatest inducements. This may be accompanied by singing. Some babies (8-12 weeks) go to sleep better if there is a light on. Soft music is sometimes helpful. A colicky baby may be outraged about being put to bed if he has had a lot of attention during the problem time. Sometimes it takes firmness for a parent to put a child to bed and let him cry. It is important to establish a bedtime pattern. Sometimes babies devise methods of their own for getting to sleep—rocking in their crib or sucking a thumb or finger.

Bedtime can be a problem for two-year-olds. A drink of water, a trip to the bathroom, one more kiss—anything to prolong going to bed is the pattern of twos. Some children are more demanding than others. What the child really wants is his mother's or father's continued presence, not the things he asks for. Ways to handle this problem: (1) Anticipate demands and take care of them in advance—drink, toilet, favorite toy. (2) Bid good-night and state firmly that you are not coming back. If the child has learned that you really mean what you say, he will usually settle down. He may call out once or twice, but with no response he will go to sleep. What if he doesn't? Many times it helps for the other parent to intervene.

As with his other behavior patterns, the two-and-a-half-year-old has his ways about sleep too! What he did yesterday, he wants to do today—and he remembers! Going-to-bed rituals have to be the same—bath, pre-bedtime play, drink, good-night—all in the same order. He may want to arrange his belongings in a certain way or take certain things to bed. A parent can be more patient with a child's rituals when he knows that this is natural for the age and stage of growth. Try to keep bedtime as simple as possible. Avoid building up a complicated ritual which your child will insist on doing.

Robert L. Jackson

From three up to six years, bedtime problems lessen or become different. Sleep may be induced by reading and quiet music. Roughhousing should be avoided at bedtime, for many children are overly stimulated with it.

Many threes go to bed quite willingly and fall asleep easily. A four-year-old may want to look at a book and turn out his own light. A five may want a little time by himself before he goes to sleep—to color, look at a book, listen to a record, or do some other quiet activity.

Sleep problems can be difficult to understand and to handle. Some preschoolers are light, fitful, restless sleepers. They are the ones who resist sleep, who wake easily during the night, who are disturbed by fears, dreams, or physical pains.

Crying and waking activities in the night are common. Many younger babies who awaken during the night will play awhile and go back to sleep. Others need personal comforting—a little food, a bottle, a change of diapers, a comforting pat, or some rocking.

Three-year-olds may have activity in the middle of the night. One may wander around the house alone. One may play, go to the bathroom, get something to eat, or look at a book. Some children go directly to their parents' room, while others do not. Preschoolers who get up at night need to be checked on to make sure they are safe in their wanderings. This is quite a natural behavior for many—not one for punishment. Night waking often disappears around four or five years.

Getting into mother's bed can become a habit with some children. If so, it is wise to stop the practice firmly, yet gently. Parents should lift the child and put him back in his own bed. Allowing him to sleep in the parents' bed can be disastrous in later years.

Bad dreams vary. Some children react with loud screams of terror that awaken the whole household. Such children may be difficult to quiet.

By three years or earlier, some children report that they are dreaming and may tell about a dream. Around four or five years, dreaming may increase. The five is the one who is usually disturbed and disturbs others by bad dreams or night terrors. Dreams and nightmares definitely invade the sleep of many fives. They generally dream of wild animals—wolves, bears, snakes, or tigers. A child may have difficulty coming out of a dream and getting awake, even with mother at his side. Those who have severe nightmares may never become awake enough to tell what is bothering them.

Parents should be calm when quieting a child about his dream. Fives may have difficulty going back to sleep. One may need considerable soothing and the mother's presence until he is asleep.

Bad dreams lessen by age six or a little later and a child is more able to control himself about a dream.

Fears related to sleep may be simple—fear of the dark, of people hiding in the room, of shadows, or of animals chasing him. Children who have fears should be treated with sympathy and **respect. They should not be teased. Threes often fear the dark.** Plan to leave a dim light in the hall or next room or a nightlight in the child's room. A four-year-old may like to keep a small flashlight under his pillow to turn on when he needs it. Reading a good book about nighttime may help a child overcome fears. Shadows bother older children more. Parents need to be sensitive to the nighttime fears and not too harsh on their child. Remember: A child's fear is very real to him. With a little help and patience from adults a child is usually able to dispel his fears after a short time.

Naptime sometimes causes problems. Some children, by two years of age, do not take a nap every day but will play contentedly in their room for an hour or so. Napping is often a real problem by age two-and-a-half. Many are slow in getting to sleep and may go to sleep some place other than their own bed. If this happens, the child should be placed in his bed each time. When he awakens, give him the assurance and comfort he needs.

The three-year-old who naps usually goes to sleep quicker **than twos and wakes up happier. Many four- or five-year-olds** do not take naps but need more rest at night.

TOILET TRAINING

Research shows that training is not effective unless the child has developed muscles necessary for the task. Toilet training depends upon nerve connections which must mature. The nervous system develops more rapidly in some children than in others. Toilet training must wait for a certain amount of maturity in the child's central nervous system.

The danger of starting training too young is that success is taken too seriously by the mother and is expected to continue. Generally, there is no real success before two years of age. Many mothers report that their child trained himself around two years of age.

Bladder control probably has more individual differences than any other child behavior; yet it is the area in which parents are most impatient. There is no proper age for staying dry.

After the child is a year old, a mother can watch for signs that let her know when he is ready to start bowel control. He can be placed on the potty chair or toilet seat. If there are no results after five or ten minutes, the mother should take him off.

Many preschoolers, by two-and-a-half years, develop a spirit of privacy about toilet functions. They want mother to go away, and they may close the bathroom door. The child's privacy should be respected.

By three years, many children stay dry all night. Boys are slower than girls to conform to this. Picking a child up at night to go to the bathroom does not train him if he does not wake up. Waking him may do more harm than good if he has trouble going back to sleep.

Bed-wetting means more work for mother! Some children do not show any real control until six or seven years and some are eight years old before they can stay dry.

The wetting child does not want the other members of his family to know he has wet the bed. Parents help the child by honoring his wishes.

A child may achieve control at two years and then lose it at four. Increased wetting may occur during the turmoil period of five-and-a-half to six years; also, on cold nights, exciting days, or because of watching frightening TV programs.

Many psychiatrists feel that emotional factors alone are the basis of bed-wetting. No doubt emotions do have a definite part, especially in the five-to-seven-year period.

A child who does not stay dry in the daytime by three or four years of age is disturbing to the mother. She may find a time when he is apt to be dry and take him to the toilet, perhaps after a nap if he is dry then. Then she may take him to the bathroom again in a little while. Training pants may be used at a time of day when success is likely. Start slowly; do not expect too much.

Some children cannot stay dry at play! The complex task of stopping play and getting into the house in time is just too much for them. It may help to plan with the child, calling him at intervals when he plays outdoors.

The following are general suggestions about toilet training:

- Give a child the privacy he needs during elimination. Added privacy often quickly solves problems.
- A child may have bowel movements in his pants to get his mother's attention. If this is an emotional problem, there needs to be an improved mother-child relationship.
- The same span of years when the child is seeking autonomy **(18 months to 3 years) is also the time for the training period.** This is not easy for the child.
- A child has to learn the words that accompany training—the right words to say, when to say them, and how loudly he can say them. Since there are a variety of terms used relating to toileting, a parent can help the child and church teachers by telling the teachers the terminology her child knows.
- Sometimes parental discord, harsh discipline, or inconsistent discipline lie at the root of a child's difficulty. There may be a bid by the child for the love and affection of his parents. This is often the case when a baby brother or sister is born. Behavior may be the result or evidence of the child's unconscious resentment and hostility. This may be his way of getting back at parents.
- A child who is having problems in elimination should not be teased or made fun of.

SEXUAL DEVELOPMENT

Many parents feel inhibited about the idea of teaching their child about sex. Good teaching is simple and natural. Sexual education begins long before a child can ask questions. The infant's exploration of his body is part of sexual education. Observing attitudes that mothers and daddies show toward one another is part of sexual education. Toilet training, bathing, and dressing are a part of sexual education.

Children three to six want to know about their bodies; they want to know where babies come from. Five-year-olds, especially, ask questions. Lines of communication between parent and child have been growing or lessening through the years. The quality of the relationship determines the child's openness in asking questions or making comments.

Give your preschooler a good answer when he asks where

babies come from. A child wants to know only a little at the moment. Do not tell the child less than he wants to know; yet do not tell him more than he asks. He will come back with more questions if your answers satisfy him. The questions are simple and need simple, truthful answers. Threes and fours often ask: "Where do babies come from?" "How do babies get out of their mother's tummy?" By five or six years, a child usually asks: "How does a baby get (or start) inside the mother."

Masturbation is generally accepted as a normal phase of sex maturation. Usually in a happy home situation, children do not masturbate excessively and soon outgrow the habit. Brief or occasional masturbation should cause no concern. If a child continues the behavior or if it seems excessive, these actions may indicate that the child is tense or worried.

Wayne E. Oates, in his book *On Becoming Children of God,* stresses the importance of a child learning what to do with his body from the parent who has a body like his own—"imaging" himself like his father or mother. Dr. Oates feels that if children from four to six do not have wholesome "imaging" experiences, their development is hindered as will be expressed later in their religious life. "Teachers [and parents] must examine the meaning of the expanding horizons and the image of the self in terms of the Biblical perspective of this very important phase of religious life." [4] (See the above book, pages 55-64, for more detailed interpretation of the subject.)

Here are some suggestions as guidelines in helping the child have a healthy feeling about himself and sex:

• Attitudes about sex teach the child. They are more important than information about sex. Instill in the child's mind that sex is normal and natural. Parents need to strive to overcome their own inhibitions in order to present sex in a wholesome way. Sex with love is high and noble in man's experience.

• Timing of imparting information to the child is important. His questions are important.

• Take clues from the child's concern and questions. Do not present sex as a "lesson." Just answer the child's question. Do not avoid the truth. Give the child clear, honest answers to his questions.

* The child's curiosity about body differences gives parents and teachers occasion to clarify and discuss. Use correct scientific names for organs and their functions.

* Encourage the child to establish happy and wholesome attitudes about children of the opposite sex.

* The child should see in his parents a picture of happiness, contentment, satisfaction, pleasure, self-respect, respect for one's mate, and a demonstration of thoughtfulness to others in daily living.

FACT AND FANCY

The preschooler does not distinguish clearly between fact and fancy, the real and the make-believe. Around the age of two, many children start giving imaginary objects to mothers or teachers. Later they pretend they are cars, animals, TV characters. Some children even play they are babies again. Threes often invent an imaginary playmate. Fours are more aware that something is make-believe. Fives show disgust if parents do not play the make-believe game with them.

A parent can share a child's make-believe and yet let him know that he accepts it as something fanciful that did not really happen.

When reading to a child, it is helpful to let a child know when a story is true (based on facts) and when a story is just imaginary.

Later, a child may seem confused as to whether he is telling a "tall tale" or the truth. Or, he may tell a fanciful tale in order to escape the consequences of his behavior.

Asking a child "Who did this?" may make him deny having done it even if he did, especially if he recognizes by the voice that the person is upset. This may cause a child to develop a habit of telling untruths.

GUILT

From around two-and-a-half to four years of age, a child's conscience begins to develop. He begins to take some responsibility for what he does. He develops a beginning sense of guilt for an action which parents feel is not acceptable.

Because of the child's sensitive feelings with his growing conscience, it is easy for adults to make him feel guilty by impressing on him the badness of his behavior. Feeling more guilt than he can bear, the child may feel depressed and confused. He may feel less confidence in himself. He may feel resentful toward the adult who made him suffer. Unnecessary guilt can damage a personality in its early stages when one needs to develop self-esteem.

FEARS

Preschoolers grow up with assorted fears. These fears come from within and from without. When the causes are probed, one discovers that a specific fear is linked with something quite remote from it. The fear of the high chair may be traced to the time when the mother went to a hospital for a week. Babies show fear of strangers around six months of age. They detect a strangeness in an unfamiliar face. Persons who are sensitive to the young child's feelings can do much to understand and relieve a child's fears.

"The time to be concerned is not when a child has a fear. . . . We must be concerned when fear has a child." [5]

A fear of the *dark* is one of the most common and persistent fears of children. A reassuring adult needs to be present when the dark threatens children.

Fear of *dogs* is not very common and usually only temporary. A child should be allowed as much experience with dogs as he can accept. Small dogs and puppies can often be tolerated when large ones cannot. A child may accept a dog from a distance but not close. He may be able to pat a dog, if a parent is holding the dog. It is helpful to use stories and books about dogs. Also, an adult should be near the child when a dog appears.

A fear of *water* may come from being bathed, usually starting about eighteen to twenty-four months. A child may suddenly

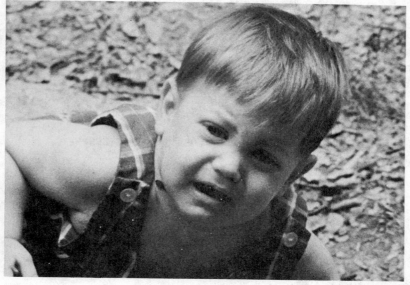

Robert L. Jackson

refuse his bath. It may be wise to give him sponge baths until the period of resistance is over. Unless a child has actually been frightened by some experience in the water, the fear may disappear easily. A five- or six-year-old may be pressured into swimming too early. A child should be allowed just to play in the water unless he shows an interest in learning to swim.

The *barbershop* is a place of fear for many children. It is helpful to allow a child to play out going to the barber before his first experience. Going with Daddy and watching him get a haircut may be a good preliminary experience for a child.

Many children fear going to the *doctor* or *dentist*. When a parent is taking a child to a doctor or dental appointment, it is essential that the parent have attitudes of cheerfulness and confidence. As a child senses his parent's attitude, his fear will likely diminish. Much of a child's fear may be overcome in role-playing the parts of dentist, doctor, or nurse.

The following summary of fears, taken from the book *Child Behavior*,[6] may be helpful:

2 years: Many fears, chiefly auditory, as trains, trucks, thunder, flushing of toilet, vacuum cleaner.

Visual fears: dark colors, large objects, trains, hats.

Spatial: toy or crib moved from usual place, moving to a new house, fear of going down the drain.

Personal: mother's departure, or separation from her at bedtime. Rain and wind.

Animals—especially wild animals.

2½ years: Many fears, especially spatial: fear of movement or of having objects moved.

Any different orientation, as someone entering house by a different door.

Large objects—as trucks—approaching.

3 years: Visual fears predominate: colored or wrinkled people, masks, "bogeymen."

The dark.

Animals.

Policemen, burglars.

Mother or father going out at night.

4 years: Auditory fears again, especially fire engines.

The dark.

Wild animals.

Mother leaving, especially going out at night.

5 years: Not a fearful age. More visual fears than others.

Less fear of animals, bad people, bogeymen.

Concrete, down-to-earth fears: bodily harm, fallings, dogs.

The dark.

That mother will not return home.

6 years: Very fearful. Especially auditory fears: doorbell, telephone, static, ugly voice tones, flushing of toilet, insect and bird noises.

Fear of supernatural: ghosts, witches,

Fear that someone is hiding under the bed.

Spatial: fear of being lost, fear of the woods.

Fear of the elements: fire, water, thunder, lightning.

Fear of sleeping alone in a room or of being only one on a floor of the house.

Fear that mother will not be home when he arrives home, or that something will happen to her or that she may die.

Afraid others will hit him.

Brave about big hurts but fears splinters, little cuts, blood, nose drops.

In handling children's fears, being prepared for the unexpected is most important. The child withdraws from things which are, or seem, dangerous or harmful to him. The period may be long or short, depending on the child, the situation, and the parent's reaction. The child's natural tendency to withdraw from things he fears should be respected. Many times a child gets over his fear without help. Things look different as he grows older. He understands more. The idea that continually exposing a child to the thing he fears is a good way to get him over the fear is not a good way.

Attitudes and unthoughtful remarks by adults may prompt unnecessary fears for a child. Threats used as disciplinary measures, such as "The policeman will get you if you do that," are unfair to the child.

It is wise to build caution in children to help them become aware of real dangers, but cautions need to be given with a calm, quiet approach.

Parents should not pretend that fears do not exist or that they should not exist. A child's fears should be acknowledged and accepted. When a child has expressed his fears, he can manage them better.

A child who is afraid needs the support of parents and teachers. He does not need a rebuff or unkind words. He needs adults to give him strength he does not have. When parents hold back their support from the child, his fears mount.

Minor fears that have been instilled, ignored, or made light of, pile up within the child so that he becomes afraid—not of dogs, or water, or trains—but of life. He becomes less curious, less adventurous, less at ease in the world.

Parents may help their preschooler overcome fears by:

- Respecting his fears.
- Allowing him reasonable periods to withdraw from fear before helping him adjust.
- Comforting him immediately (bad dreams, thunder).
- Teaching him techniques for coping with situations which are about to come up.

NEW SITUATIONS

Attending church may be a new situation for a preschooler. As a parent takes him to his department, he should observe the

Pine Lake Farm

child's reaction to new places and experiences.

The child who can meet the new and unfamiliar has a real advantage. The extreme is the child who has a tantrum when he has to deal with the new and the strange, who cannot adjust in a new place, who always shies away from strangers.

The way in which different children react to the new is usually established early in life. The vigorous child adjusts quickly and easily to the new. The less active and milder ones move in easily but quietly. Some children have initial hesitation with something unfamiliar. They have real problems with the new. When a child is going into a new place, his mother or father may hold his hand until the child lets go. A parent may point out a child or an adult which their child already knows or point to a familiar toy.

Parents should not be disappointed if their preschooler does not respond warmly and quickly to strangers or unfamiliar places. They should accept the fact that it takes their child longer than some others. They should give him as much help as possible about feeling at home in new situations.

If a child's reactions to the new are persistently negative, he needs a helping hand. Forcing him to move before he is ready imposes too much pressure and may cause the child to become more shy and afraid to try anything new. A child almost screams at us, "Don't push me!"

Be patient with the child who is slow to warm up. Do not compare him with other children. He needs to be given encouragement and allowed to take his time.

Sometime between one and two years of age, a child suddenly is keenly aware of separation from parents. If parents and other adults associated with the child's experience handle the situation calmly and with assurance, the child will soon overcome this fear.

It is difficult on a child if he is left too long and too often in group situations that are overly stimulating, tiresome, and perhaps unpleasant. A child may build up resentment for being left under such conditions. Refer to Part II, pages 89-90, about difficult times at church and review ways parents and workers can help the child in adjusting to new experiences.

BITING

Biting is in many children a short-lived way of behaving. The behavior is used when the child is in a social situation which is too difficult for him. He seems to be unable to find a way to express himself effectively, so he resorts to biting.

What can be done about the behavior? If possible, simplify the play situation. Allow him to play with only a few children at a time and with children with whom he enjoys playing. The child needs to have good adult supervision. Anticipate the biting and interfere before the act occurs. Help the child find more expressive ways to satisfy his feelings. If a child can be kept away from situations that are too difficult, the urge to bite soon disappears.

In a group situation, if there is one child who persists in biting, have one teacher follow the child around for a morning or two. If the child can be prevented from biting for a session or two, he will probably stop.

When biting continues over a period of time, then consider

that it is a sign of defense mechanism being used because of some emotional difficulty.

Sucking represents a powerful drive in the very young. Preschoolers enjoy it, and it should not be regarded as a bad habit. Thumb-sucking is normal during the first two years of life. Efforts to break it may cause resentment and a sense of frustration, and the habit may continue longer than it normally would.

A baby has an innate urge to do a certain amount of sucking. If he does not get it in obtaining food, he is likely to continue sucking by using his thumb. Thumb-sucking may indicate that the baby is not getting enough of the right kind of food, or it may occur because a child is not getting enough rest.

If a child continues thumb-sucking beyond age two-and-a-half, it is no longer because of the simple need to suck. It is a source of comfort and satisfaction to the child—perhaps a symptom of an emotional need. The persistent thumb-sucker may be a lonely or bored child. He is often an insecure child. There is a need to look for causes in the child's home life—parental quarreling, indifference to the child, inconsistent discipline, harsh discipline, favoritism of one parent to one child. Adequate steps should be taken to meet the child's need of love and affection.

When thumb-sucking continues after age five, this indicates something is wrong in the child's world. There is real reason to consult a doctor or to check at a child guidance clinic.

Generally, parents should not make an issue of a child's sucking his thumb. Most children give up the habit before they go to school. Nagging, shaming, bribing, and punishing a child who sucks his thumb will only make matters worse, because these methods bring added unhappiness.

Give attention to the child's emotional well-being. Nervous habits of this kind are not likely to develop in a child whose home life is serene and happy. A child needs love, security, attention, and a happy home.

Jealousy is an emotional reaction common in most children. It is a powerful force in motivating a child's behavior. It is significant in his adjustment and the adjustment of those around him.

The arrival of a new baby in the home may bring jealousy and hurt. A new baby is a threat to the child's security. The child has difficulty sharing his mother's love. The young child probably has little understanding of the feelings he harbors or of the reasons for their existence.

When the preschooler is aware of the expected birth, parents have plenty of time to answer questions and to include the child in plans and preparation for the new family member. Even with this, there may be many unasked questions and unexpressed worries.

In talking with a child about the coming of the baby, let him know that at times mother will be busy with the baby but that he will be able to help too. Help him feel that it takes everyone in the family to make a happy home.

Parents need to assume that jealousy exists in children, even though it is not always visible. A child wants to be the only object of his parents' love, so jealousy can never be totally prevented. When children repress jealousy, it comes out in disguised ways in behavior patterns adults may not understand. For example: If a child does not speak his resentment, he may dream that he does something dangerous to the baby. He may wake up screaming. It is better if a child expresses his resentment in words rather than a nightmare.[7]

Some symptoms of jealousy are coughing, skin rashes, bed-wetting, nail-biting, or destructiveness.

Age and sex differences may cause jealousy among siblings. If rivalry leads to deep resentment and jealous reactions, the effects will likely be negative. A child then builds a defense of his own to deal with his hurt. His jealous reaction may be direct or hidden. The indirect reaction is difficult to understand and to handle. At the core of jealousy is the fundamental feeling of having been deprived of favorable status with a loved person because of the existence of someone else. A child may be jealous of his father for his mother's affection. Since affection seems to be basic in the matter, adults need to provide the kind of affection that is appropriate for the child.

In dealing with the problem of jealousy, remember:

- Punishment and insult will not stop the child's feelings.
- An older child should not be allowed to bully his brother or sister.
- Older and younger children do not need to be treated alike. Age should bring new privileges and new responsibilities.
- One child should not be asked to make sacrifices for another.

TEMPER TANTRUMS

An occasional tantrum may be expected in any child up to age six or seven. If a child has a tantrum every day or several times a day, parents have a serious problem.

Causes of tantrums.—Children differ innately in their ability to tolerate frustration and in their tendency toward irritability. A temper tantrum is not inherited, but learned. A child may imitate tantrums of his father, since he is apt to identify himself with his father's behavior and attitudes. A parent needs to set a pattern for the child. Temper problems are likely to occur in a child who is tired, hungry, or unwell. Too harsh and too repressive discipline often contribute to temper tantrums. A child may be in need of companionship and attention. A tantrum may be a sign of inner panic, resentment, loneliness, or a feeling of rejection or neglect.

A common question is: What shall I do when a child has a temper tantrum?

- Punishment is not the answer, for the child is putting himself through enough punishment. In case of insecurity, punishment will only increase the insecurity. The child needs more love and attention.
- When the tantrum occurs, a child should be taken to a quiet place with an understanding and sympathetic adult. A child needs security when he loses control of himself. In addition, a tantrum is not very satisfying without an audience.
- It is useless to try to reason with a child during a tantrum. When the tantrum is over, you may need to soothe the child, for he is afraid of his own violence and anger. Talk about something unrelated to the experience which resulted in the tantrum.

• Avoid trying to appease a child, or he may conclude that such action will get him what he wants. Children try various ways of meeting frustration difficulty and in getting their way. If a child finds that a tantrum brings what he wants, he is almost bound to use this as a way of controlling his parents.

Sometimes children are pushed too hard.

PREJUDICE

Prejudice is not inherited; it is caught through environmental influences. Fours and fives may develop at least a degree of prejudice, depending on the attitudes which they detect in people important to them. They may feel prejudice about religious groups, social status, or race.

Children have the ability to recognize deep feelings. A child's attitudes are nourished by what he absorbs in day-by-day events around him. Facial expressions, tone of voice, expression in eyes, and physical gestures of adults can convey prejudice as distinctly as the spoken word.

Parents and teachers should use every possible occasion to extend the child's horizon about all humanity. Adults may lead children to have the concept that all people are interesting, important, and valuable.

3. CRISES IN A PRESCHOOLER'S LIFE

Wallowitch

Not every preschooler will meet with a real crisis, but those who do will have difficult adjustments. Parents and teachers need to try to understand how the child feels and find ways to help him cope with whatever problems may result for him. Parents can help the child and the church by informing the child's teachers of crises that occur. The church can be helpful to the entire family if the leaders are aware of an existing problem.

DEATH

A child early in life knows something about death because of contact with dead animals, insects, and birds. However, a preschooler does not perceive death as adults do.

For many children, the first death in the family may be that of a grandparent. A child may experience death in the passing of a close family friend or a neighbor.

Parents need to talk with the child about death when it is a part of the child's experience. The manner and attitude in which a parent approaches death are more important than the words. The child will be more sensitive to the parent's feelings than to the facts of death.

The child from birth to about four years can sense the loss of a person, but he cannot comprehend death. A child may have weird interpretations about death when his limited understanding of facts becomes mixed up with his feelings. His feelings call for love, reassurance, and emotional support. His feelings are much deeper than adults realize. A four- or five-year-old will be interested in the biological aspects of death. He will want to know what is done with the body of the deceased. He may ask why people are buried in the ground.

Parents often ask: "Should I take my child to his grandfather's funeral?" Edgar N. Jackson, in his book *Telling a Child About Death*,[8] suggests that a child be allowed to attend the funeral. He should not be denied the experiences which he knows is important to the family. But, no child should be forced to attend against his wishes.

Parents do the child an injustice if they try to hide grief and disappointment in the death of a loved one or friend. Try not to deceive a child about the sad feelings which you have. Genuine emotions cannot be locked up or told to go away. A child senses the feelings in your actions and attitudes. A child may be frightened if an adult tries to hide his grief.

A child's limited experience is protection against the stress which adults feel. Share feelings at the child's level of understanding. This will help him in building his sense of trust and in a better understanding of others.

When adults try to protect a child in the time of grief, a child's grief may be worked out in behavior adults do not understand. Grief may come out in anger through noisy and boisterous behavior.

Children often ask difficult questions about death. One child asked: "Why did God let my granddaddy die?" Perhaps an answer such as, "Because his body got worn out" is enough for a child under four. Fours and fives may be told about accidents or illnesses without becoming too disturbed.

"Where do dead people go?" is another common question. Questions give adults an opportunity to explain God's plan about life and death for all living things. It is important to help the child understand that God is not unjust, that he knows best what is right in all things. We do not always understand why things happen, but we know God is taking care of the world and all people.

The child is threatened by death because it is unknown and it happens to people. He feels it may happen to him.

LOSS OF A PET

It is a heartbreaking experience for a young child to lose a pet, whether the loss is by death or simply disappearance. If a pet has disappeared from the home, parents should make every effort to help their child locate the pet.

A young child cannot comprehend that death is permanent. Death makes a child feel weak and anxious. He sees that in spite of all his tears and protests, his pet is no longer with him. The child is disappointed and feels abandoned.

A child should not be deprived of the right to mourn over the loss of a pet. He should be free to feel and express his sorrow. If a dog or cat is hit by a car, parents should not try to protect their child from the truth. Allow the child to bury the pet in whatever way he desires, giving him the assistance he needs.

A four- or five-year-old may ask if his pet has gone to heaven. Adults should avoid trying to make things easier by answering in the affirmative. We have no indications that pets do go to heaven. The child needs understanding and consolation at such times. One childhood educator has offered this suggestion in answer to this type of anxiety from the child: "God has made dogs and cats and all other living things. When an animal dies, God has made some kind of provision for the animal that we know must be best, even though we do not know what it is. We can trust God to take care of all the things that he has created."

When a pet dies, some parents hurry to replace it with a new one. Should we give the child the idea that love can be transferred this easily? Regardless of how pretty or expensive the substitute pet may be, it will probably be some time before the child's love and interest can be related to the new pet.

ILLNESS

A child most likely will experience minor illness several times while he is a preschooler. He may also have experiences of his mother or other members in the family being ill. If the mother is very ill, this may necessitate having some adult come

to the home, at least in the daytime, during the illness. If there are relatives nearby, they may be in a position to help. During a mother's illness, the child needs to have extra love and assurance that everything will be all right as Mother receives the care she needs for recovery.

A preschooler may become ill with a contagious disease. This may not be a serious experience, though it may be uncomfortable for him. If a child is ill in the home, he needs careful attention. If necessary, a doctor's help should be secured to diagnose the illness. Attention must be given to the basic consideration of rest, diet, elimination, treatment, and convalescent period. The child needs to understand that medicine must be taken because it speeds his recovery. The hardest days usually are the ones when a child is recovering and may be in his room and about the home but unable to go outside. A mother can help the child engage in many activities that will be interesting, but these will vary in accordance with the child's age and illness.

Most doctors recommend that surgery for a child be postponed until the child is at least three and a half years old, and if possible, until he is six. If a child must be hospitalized during his preschool years, careful plans should be made and shared with the child.

- Take the child to meet the surgeon so that he may gain the child's trust and confidence.
- Explain to your child the reason for the operation in simple words.
- Explain that a certain amount of pain is unavoidable.
- If the hospital is near, show your child the hospital. Otherwise, show him pictures of a hospital, nurses, and doctors.
- Read a book such as *Johnny Goes to the Hospital* or *Randy Visits the Doctor*.
- Explain how anesthesia is used (if you feel your child is old enough to understand anything about the procedure).

Both parents should be at the hospital with the child before and after the operation. Many hospitals now have the mother stay with the sick child. She is allowed to do many of the routine nursing jobs. The support of the mother's presence lessens fear within the child. A child may cry more when the mother is there, but he is less frightened.

The child needs frequent visits from both parents. He needs the assurance and confidence that he feels when they are nearby.

DIVORCED PARENTS

"In the United States . . . one marriage in four ends in divorce. . . . Experts predict that within a few years one marriage in three in the United States will terminate in divorce. At present for every four divorces, three children are involved."[9]

More women than men have the responsibility for rearing children, because courts usually award children to the mother. Most children of divorce, therefore, are deprived of the father influence needed in their lives.

Dr. David Goodman reports that the largest number of rejected children in the United States is the army of orphans of divorce. There are 4,000,000 of them now and the number may grow in time to 10,000,000.[10]

Divorce, to even the young child, may be a baffling experience since his mother, his daddy, and his home are the only world he knows. The child wants and needs both parents *together.* Divorce may cause suffering and humiliation to a child. He may lack for many rights and privileges that other children enjoy. He may feel rejected and bitter. Nothing that is given to the divorce-orphaned child can make up for the normal family life with two parents who love him and each other.

The usual divorce gives little thought to the emotional needs of children, but the spiritual and emotional life of a child can be greatly blighted by divorce. A child requires masculine and feminine influence in his development. The lack of this balance may cause personality distresses. Divorce can be tragic for a child!

Churches can help the child of divorce by having men as teachers in the departments for young children. This father influence, for even a brief time on Sunday, may help fulfill the child's need for the masculine relationship if he is in custody of his mother.

REMARRIAGE OF A PARENT

The remarriage may be because of the death of a mate or because of divorce.

A wise new parent recognizes the variety of attitudes and experiences the child may bring to the new relationship. If the child's parent has died, there may have been a long illness with a consequent atmosphere of tension and anxiety in the home. If parents were divorced, this involved a period of disagreeing and quarreling, giving the child a sense of insecurity. If both of the parents are living, the child is apt to have a conflict of loyalties. Whatever feelings the child has, they may be revealed in his behavior.

The child is faced with accepting the new parent and establishing a new relationship. There may be other children in the marriage to whom the child must adjust.

The natural parent should help prepare the child for the parent's marriage. The prospective new parent should attempt to win the regard and affection of the child. Parents must understand the experience through which the child has gone. They **must keep in mind what is normally involved in behavior as** children grow. They must be prepared to accept behavior patterns which may appear because of adjustments the child is making. The child will need to have adequate love, understanding, acceptance, and assurance from parents.

ECONOMIC FAILURE

The number of people living in poverty at the end of 1967 in America was 29 million. During the summer of 1968 there were 476,173 children enrolled in Head Start, a program to help prepare preschoolers for entrance into school. During 1968, more than 250,000 members of seasonally employed agricultural workers' families were reached by education, day care, and housing programs.[11]

A look at the above figures helps adults realize that many preschoolers today are living under the blight of economic failure. Even the very young child has some concept of how society is maintained. He is aware that his father works. An older preschooler knows that Daddy makes money so that the family can have food, clothing, a home, and other necessary items for living. When a father loses his job or his business, the child may be frightened and feel insecure. If a family remains in this position for long, a child develops the feeling of failure and rejection. His feelings may cause antisocial behavior.

A family with economic problems presents the church with **an opportunity to minister. Preschoolers from such homes need understanding teachers who can give them the needed help.**

WAR

The threat of war today touches all children—of different races and from diverse economic and social levels.

There has not been a time since World War II when parents of preschoolers in America have not been involved in military service. Many fathers have served in reserve groups as well as in active duty.

Today, many preschoolers and their mothers are living alone while fathers are in military service. Many fathers are out of the United States, and some children have not seen their father for months or perhaps a year or more; some will never see their fathers.

What emotional feelings do preschoolers experience in the absence of a father as he is involved in war? Perhaps the deepest feeling is that of fear, particularly if the child is three or older. A strong fear of the child is that of losing a parent. The child may also experience loneliness, insecurity, and anxiety. Even with the best possible efforts of a mother to partly take the place of the absent father, she cannot supply the need of the child for his father.

THE HANDICAPPED CHILD

A handicapped child is one "who has a generally recognized and persistent physical or mental defect which prevents him from taking part freely in the activities that are so important to all children," says Herbert Stolz.[12] He also states that *"only very rarely is either of the parents responsible for the child's handicap."* [13]

Handicaps include loss of vision, hearing, crippling deformity, damage to the heart or nervous system, and severe mental and emotional difficulties.

Parents should accept the handicapped child as their child, without shame, resentment, pity, guilt, or resignation. A child needs to feel secure in the love of his parents, to have a sense of personal worth, and to grow in independence and achievement. He needs inspiration to rally his resources of body and mind to make something of himself. Full acceptance is the first step in helping the child make progress.

The parents' goal should be to help the handicapped child get the best out of life. The level of functioning which the child can achieve depends on several factors: the nature and severity of the defect, the effectiveness of medical treatment and rehabilitation, the attitude and approach of parents, the characteristics of the child, and the use of special facilities available for the child's development.

The responsibilities of parents of the handicapped are demanding and complex. They need to listen to instructions of specialists and follow them explicitly. They must not overprotect the child from demands he is capable of meeting. They must wait for the child to succeed through many failures and disappointments. They have to be shields from situations with which he cannot cope.

Parents who feel shame and guilt make the mistake of giving excessive devotion to the child. This is not good for the handicapped child. It is also bad for other children in the family.

The handicapped child needs to be protected while he learns to function independently as much as possible. The more he learns to get along on his own, the healthier his emotional development and the more normal his life. Many handicapped children, guided in the right way, can more than compensate for their initial handicaps.

Diseases or mishaps which occur before or during birth or in childhood cause retardation. Research indicates that many mentally retarded children improve intellectually with age. A child considered almost hopeless at any early age may turn out a far better adult than was anticipated.

Much has been accomplished through research, medical science, and education in recent years to improve the plight of mentally handicapped children. Today increasing facilities are being provided to enable the retarded child to develop in accordance with his own needs and capacities.

Many churches today are making special provision for retarded children through a separate class or inclusion with other groups of children. They search for a teacher who has accepted the retarded child and is interested in his development.

THE GIFTED CHILD

The "gifted" child is usually considered the one who is academically gifted, though a person may be "gifted" in areas of music, art, drama, and other areas. Performance is one of the best indications of giftedness. If a child is clearly ahead of other children his age in performance, he may be gifted.

Parents need to be aware of their gifted child's abilities and capacities in order to give him wise guidance. Parents need to see that their gifted child grows up with good habits of thinking, good work habits, and an enthusiasm for learning.

A gifted child may teach himself to read by age five. Gifted children usually like to talk and discuss. They show intellectual curiosity, ask relevant questions, are quick to learn, are good at solving problems, and have an extraordinary memory.

In most schools today, attention is given to the gifted child. Some type of program usually exists in the school system of a town or city so that the gifted can have acceleration and enrichment in his curriculum. The gifted child needs to have a broad knowledge of history and civilization.

The gifted child needs to be challenged so that his drives and goals are met. His unusual gifts can lead to emotional problems if his intellectual capacity is not stimulated and inspired.

Usually, churches are far behind the schools in ministry to gifted children. Churches need to recognize that they have a responsibility and stewardship to the gifted. Churches have a ministry to offer gifted children that other institutions and agencies do not have.

The gifted person has ethical understandings and spiritual insights and concerns. His idealism may seek expression through experiences in the church.

THE "CHOSEN" CHILD

"Shall I tell my child he is adopted?" Most adoptive parents realize that it is of utmost importance to tell a child at the earliest possible moment that he is a chosen child. This procedure is the only solid foundation for the security of the child and his parents. One pediatrician has suggested that parents tell the child about his adoption as soon as he begins to ask for stories.[14] Parents may read a book to the child about an adopted child, such as *The Pretty House That Found Happiness* by Eisenberg. Parents should feel free to share with teachers and others about the child's adoption.

Parents should avoid referring to the child's adoption constantly, or he may feel insecure. Parents must not get the idea that when a child misbehaves it is due to bad heredity.

Parents must treat the child as their own. They should never make the child feel that they are sorry they adopted him. They must accept the child as he is and help him to be his best self.

Adoptive parents are the real parents. The strangers who produced the child are only biological parents.

Growing

When I ask Mother
she doesn't really know:
"What's inside of me
making me grow?"

So I ask Father
who doesn't grow a bit:
"What's inside of YOU
making you quit?"

And Father says, "Hmmm . . .
"I'm — busy — now, Son . . ."
So I STILL don't know
how growing is done.[15]

---

1. Frances L. Ilg and Louise Bates Ames, *Child Behavior* (New York: Dell Publishing Co., 1955) , p. 118.

2. *Ibid.*, p. 17.

3. *Ibid.*, p. 95.

4. Wayne E. Oates, *On Becoming Children of God* (Philadelphia: The Westminister Press, 1969), p. 55.

5. James L. Hymes, Jr., *The Child Under Six* (Englewood Cliffs, New Jersey: Prentice-Hall, Inc., 1967) , p. 241.

6. Ilg and Ames, *op. cit.*, pp. 172–74.

7. Haim G. Ginott, *Between Parent and Child* (New York: Avon Books, 1965), pp. 146–52.

8. Edgar N. Jackson, *Telling a Child About Death* (New York: Channel Press, 1965), pp. 28–33.

9. David Goodman, *A Parents' Guide to the Emotional Needs of Children* (New York: Hawthorn Books, Inc., 1969) , pp. 103–4.

10. *Ibid.*, p. 99.

11. *The 1969 World Book Year Book* (Chicago: Field Enterprises Educational Corporation 1969, pp. 456–61.

12. Sidonie Matsner Gruenberg, *The New Encyclopedia of Child Care and Guidance* (Rev. Ed., Garden City, New York: Doubleday and Company, Inc., 1968), p. 965.

13. *Ibid.*, p. 966.

14. Morton Edwards, *Your Child—Today* (New York: Permabook, 1960), pp. 66–68.

15. "Growing," from *In One Door and Out the Other,* by Aileen Fisher. Copyright © 1969 by Thomas Y. Crowell Company, New York, publishers, and reprinted with their permission.

Contents to Part IV

Part IV

You Can Help

1. ARE YOU READY?

As you live and work with preschoolers, are you ready to help

The tiny baby?
The toddler?
The two-year-old?
The three-year-old?
The four-year-old?
The five-year-old?
The six-year-old not yet in school?

You have read (and studied?):

1. The Preschooler Is a Person
2. The Preschooler in Today's World
3. Facing Today with the Preschooler

Your interest in reading this book is an indication that you want to understand preschoolers, that you want to help today's preschoolers who are looking to you and the other adults in his life for love and guidance. The preschooler needs you to help him become the personality he is capable of becoming.

No two children are alike . . . each child has his very special qualities . . . each child's experiences are different from every other child . . . each child differs in intelligence, his rate of growth, his depth of feelings . . . each child has strengths, weaknesses, potentials, blind spots . . . each child leads a different life.

2. DO YOU REMEMBER?

We try to understand each child for what he was, what he is, and what he can become. With this in view, let's review some of the overall needs, interests, crises, and understandings of preschoolers presented in this book.

The preschooler has basic needs that must be met in order that he may grow and achieve selfhood. He needs:

love	acceptance	security
a sense of trust	control	self-respect
dependence and independence		guidance

This preschooler is different from every other individual because of nature and nurture. His growth is influenced by the interaction of hereditary and environmental forces constantly at work within and around him.

This person's development gives evidence of law and order. No two children grow exactly alike, but there is sequence in development. Each stage of *growth* is an outgrowth of the one preceding it. Each stage of *thinking* is an outgrowth of the one preceding it. The rate of development is not constant—sometimes fast, sometimes slow. A child revises his behavior as he proceeds from one stage to the next.

The growth patterns and changes occur from stage to stage

until a child is six years old. Areas of growth cannot be separated. Physical, mental, emotional, social, spiritual, and developmental tasks are interwoven in a preschooler's total development.

Perhaps one of the most important things observed is that through all the child's growth and change, his basic needs call for understanding and guidance from parents and teachers and other adults associated with the child.

Three major developmental tasks (or, as Reuel Howe calls them, objectives of love) of the preschooler strongly influence the child's goal of achieving selfhood. Unless he has satisfaction in attaining these goals during his first five years, his chances of selfhood will be hampered. The tasks are:

1. A sense of trust
2. A sense of autonomy (independence)
3. A sense of initiative

Intellectual development is a part of the child's total growth. He learns! How does he learn?

- Through relationships with adults
- Through the senses
- By imitating
- Through curiosity
- Through repetition
- By doing
- Through play
- Through satisfaction

The child learns spiritual values at church and at home. He forms concepts of:

God	**Natural World**
Jesus	**Family**
Bible	**Others**
Church	**Self**

The preschooler today lives in a society that is different from the one in which adults of today grew up. There are serious problems in the child's world, and they will continue to affect the child's life as he develops. He lives in the midst of:

violence	demonstrations	vandalism
overcrowded schools	war	juvenile delinquency
immorality	race riots	drug addicts
smog	divorce	overcrowded cities

He becomes aware of some of the problems.

———

The child is living in the midst of many advances and advantages which will continue to change living patterns for him as he grows:

space exploration	atomic age	miracle drugs
heart and kidney transplants	automation	prosperity
computers	warnings against cigarettes	

———

The scientific and technological revolutions have brought increasing pressures upon society. It has become the compulsion of many parents to try to speed up the growth of their children. Academic acceleration has dropped below the level of school age—and there is much pressure to teach the preschooler to read—a skill for which he is not ready.

———

The rapid pace of life in general has brought pressure on family living. There seems to be no time for relaxed family life when each one enjoys the other.

Many preschoolers are being affected (for good and bad) by the widespread use of television where, in many cases, there is little or no supervision.

Many preschoolers today are insecure and lonely because of increasing mobility of population from one part of the country to another.

Race problems take form in various ways, and the preschooler is much aware of it because of what he learns through television, home conversation, day schools, and church.

A normal home life does not exist for a host of young children because of working mothers and absentee fathers.

———

Many preschoolers are receiving a degree of compensation from the constant pressures and disrupted home life through opportunities which they have in group-living experiences of various forms. Many educators and childhood specialists today feel that it is a distinct advantage for a preschooler to have the benefits of a good nursery school and kindergarten before he is six years old. The opportunity for personal relationships with other young children, under skilled guidance, makes a real contribution to the preschooler's social development. The child also gains in motor control and development and in intellectual faculties as he is actively engaged in the use of appropriate and challenging equipment and materials.

———

Preschoolers have group-living experiences in other situations, the effects of which may be measured from excellent to poor. Parents need to investigate carefully any situation before exposing their child to the experiences which he may have. Some of the places where preschoolers experience group-living are:

church   nursery school   kindergarten

day care centers   playgrounds and parks

public nurseries   baby-sitters

grandparents or other relative in the home

———

When preschoolers have problems, they need help! They need parents and teachers who do not punish them for their behavior, adults who must look to discover the child's source of anxiety, fear, or whatever his emotional problem may be. They need adults who recognize that children with problems are really children with "troubles"—there is something wrong in the child's life and his world that needs to be put in order.

Some days are not good for the preschooler. Something goes wrong! Life is not void of problems, even in the first five years. Every child is bound to have problems—some rather common, others more complex. Preschoolers have trouble with:

fears	toileting	sex	sleeping
fact and fancy		eating	guilt
"Who am I?"		"Who are you?"	

or perhaps more complicated problems, like biting, thumb-sucking, jealousy, tantrums, and prejudice.

A preschooler's task: *facing problems.*

Once in a while a real crisis comes in the life of a preschooler, and it is then that he needs an added amount of love and assurance. A child may experience:

Death of a family member or family friend
Loss of a pet
Illness (himself or a member of the family)
Divorce of parents
Remarriage of a parent
Economic failure of family
War (with father involved)
Being a handicapped child
Being a gifted child
Being a "chosen" child

Each child is a person, striving each day toward selfhood. He needs adults who love and understand to guide him in achieving his goal.

3. TODAY—WHAT WILL YOU DO?

The child's goal, selfhood, is dependent upon his achievement of self-esteem.

As he feels that others see him, so he will be.

As he sees himself—worthy and confident, or worthless and confused—so he sees his neighborhood.

As he sees his neighborhood, so he sees the world.

Let us see how children of the slums would say it, children who are Negro or Puerto Rican:

On "How I See Myself": (age 13)

"Sometimes I feel as if somebody is always talking about me. I feel as if I weren't wanted. When I walk down the street, the kids are always yelling as they play. There are also some dogs." [1]

On "How I See My Neighborhood": (age 14)

"Snowflakes fall with grace
And cover city's dirt
Why do you leave soon?" [2]

On "The World Outside": (age 7)

" . . . and make peace too
and keep new york city good too
and make peace too and stop the
war toys" [3]

4. HOW MUCH WILL YOU STUDY?

Church Study Course Books

To supplement a teacher's and parent's overall picture of the preschooler, two books are written to parallel the book *Understanding Preschoolers.*

PRESCHOOLERS AT CHURCH
by
Eugene Chamberlain, Robert A. Harty, and Saxe Adams

This book offers help in organizing and equipping a department at church to provide appropriately for preschoolers.

GUIDING PRESCHOOLERS
by
Florence Conner Hearn

This book will help you know how to guide preschoolers in your church and in the home.

Periodicals

Basic guidance and teaching suggestions for preschoolers are given in the curriculum magazines. The magazine for parents of preschoolers* is planned to enrich parents' understanding and guidance of children. It is based on a Christian approach to living.

Guide A for Preschool Teachers (teachers of babies, creepers, toddlers—Sunday School and Church Training)
Guide B for Preschool Teachers (teachers of twos and threes—Sunday School and Church Training)
Guide C for Preschool Teachers (teachers of fours and fives—Sunday School and Church Training)
The Music Leader (teachers of fours and fives—Church Music)
Start (teachers of babies, toddlers, twos, threes, fours, and fives—Women's Missionary Union)
*Living with Preschoolers (parents of preschoolers)

Resource Materials

A wide variety of viewpoints are expressed in these materials. Although no one reader will agree with all of the viewpoints expressed, the materials should be stimulating to those who continually seek to understand the preschooler.

Books

Arnold, Arnold. *Teaching Your Child to Learn from Birth to School Age*. Englewood Cliffs, New Jersey: Prentice-Hall, Inc., 1971.
Axline, Virginia M. *Dibs: In Search of Self*. New York: Ballantine Books, 1964.
Baker, Katherine Read, and Xenia F. Fane. *Understanding and Guiding Young Children*. Englewood Cliffs, New Jersey: Prentice-Hall, Inc., 1967.
Carlson, Bernice Wells, and David R. Ginglend. *Play Activities for the Retarded Child*. New York: Abingdon Press, 1961.
Chandler, Caroline, Reginald S. Lourie, and Anne DeHuff Peters. *Early Child Care: The New Perspectives*. New York: Atherton Press, 1968.

Chess, Stella, Alexander Thomas, and Herbert G. Birch. *Your Child Is a Person.* New York: Parallax, 1965.

Church, Joseph. *Understanding Your Child from Birth to Three.* New York: Random House, 1973.

Dinkmeyer, Don, and Rudolph Dreikurs. *Encouraging Children to Learn.* Englewood Cliffs, New Jersey: Prentice-Hall, Inc., 1963.

Dodson, Fitzhugh. *How to Parent.* Los Angeles: Nash Publishing Co., 1970.

Dreikurs, Rudolf, and Vicki Soltz. *Children: The Challenge.* New York: Duell, Sloan and Pearce, 1964.

Erikson, Erik H. *Childhood and Society.* Rev. Ed., New York: W. W. Norton and Company, Inc., 1968.

Fraiberg, Selma H. *The Magic Years.* New York: Charles Scribner's Sons, 1965.

Fremon, Suzanne Strait. *Children and Their Parents.* New York: Harper and Row, Publishers, Inc., 1968.

Gardner, D. Bruce. *Development in Early Childhood.* New York: Harper and Row, 1964.

Ginott, Haim G. *Between Parent and Child.* New York: The Macmillan Company, 1965.

Goldman, Ronald. *Religious Thinking from Childhood to Adolescence.* New York: Seabury Press, Inc., 1968.

Goodman, David. *A Parents' Guide to the Emotional Needs of Children.* New York: Hawthorn Books, Inc., 1968.

Goodman, Mary Ellen. *Race Awareness in Young Children.* New York: Collier Books, 1964.

Gordon, Ira J. *Baby Learning Through Baby Play* (a Parent's Guide for the First Two Years) New York: St. Martin's Press, 1972.

Gordon. Ira J. *Child Learning Through Child Play* (Learning Activities for Two- and Three-Year-Olds) . New York: St. Martin's Press, 1970.

Gowan, John C. and George D. Demos (eds.). *Guidance of Exceptional Children.* New York: David McKay Co., 1965.

Grant, Wilson W. *From Parent to Child About Sex.* Grand Rapids: Zondervan Publishing House, 1973.

Gruenberg, Sidonie Matsner. *The New Encyclopedia of Child Care and Guidance.* New York: Doubleday and Company, Inc., 1968.

Hartley, Ruth E., Lawrence K. Frank, and Robert M. Goldenson. *Understanding Children's Play.* New York: Columbia University Press, 1952.

Havighurst, Robert J. *Developmental Tasks and Education.* New York: David McKay Co., Inc., 1952.

Heffernan, Helen, and Vivian E. Todd. *The Years Before School.* New York: The Macmillan Company, 1964.

Homan, William E. *Child Sense: A Pediatrician's Guide for Today's Families.* New York: Basic Books, Inc., 1969.

Howe, Reuel L. *Herein Is Love.* (Chap. 4) Valley Forge: Judson Press, 1961.

Hymes, James L., Jr. *The Child Under Six.* Englewood Cliffs, New Jersey: Prentice-Hall, Inc., 1963.

Ilg, Frances L., and Louise Bates Ames. *Child Behavior.* New York: Harper and Row, 1955.

Jackson, Edgar N. *Telling a Child About Death.* New York: Channel Press, 1965.

Jenkins, Gladys Gardner, Helen S. Schacter, and William W. Bauer. *These Are Your Children.* Atlanta: Scott, Foresman and Company, 1966.

Klink, Johanna. *Your Child and Religion.* Richmond: John Knox Press, 1971.

Koonce, Ray. *Growing with Your Children.* Nashville: Broadman Press, 1963.

LeShan, Eda J. *The Conspiracy Against Childhood.* New York: Atheneum Publishers, 1967.

Lee, Roy S. *Your Growing Child and Religion.* New York: The Macmillan Company, 1963.

Missildine, W. Hugh. *Your Inner Child of the Past.* New York: Simon and Schuster, 1963.

Murphy, Lois Barclay, et al. *The Widening World of Childhood, Paths Toward Mastery.* New York: Basic Books, Inc., 1962.

Oates, Wayne E., *On Becoming Children of God.* Philadelphia: The Westminster Press, 1969.

Piaget, Jean. *The Child's Conception of the World.* Totowa, New Jersey: Littlefield, Adams, and Company, 1960.

Pitcher, Evelyn G., and others. *Helping Young Children Learn.* Columbus: Charles E. Merrill Publishing Company, 1966.

Read, Katherine H. *The Nursery School.* 5th Ed., Philadelphia: W. B. Saunders Company, 1971.

Robertson, James (ed.). *Hospitals and Children: A Parent's Eye View.* New York: International Universities Press, Inc., 1963.

Rudolph, Marguerita, and Dorothy H. Cohen. *Kindergarten: A Year of Learning.* New York: Appleton-Century-Crofts, Inc., 1964.

Satir, Virginia. *Peoplemaking.* Palo Alto, California: Science and Behavior Books, Inc., 1972.

Smart, Mollie S. and Russell C. *Children Development and Relationships.* New York: The Macmillan Company, 1967.

Torrance, E. Paul. *Education and the Creative Potential.* Minneapolis: University of Minnesota Press, 1963.

Wallach, Michael A., and Nathan Kogan. *Modes of Thinking in Young Children.* New York: Holt, Rinehart and Winston, Inc., 1965.

Wickes, Frances G. *Inner World of Childhood.* Rev. Ed., New York: New American Library, Inc., 1968.

Young, Leontine R. *Life Among the Giants.* New York: McGraw-Hill Book Company, 1966.

Wolf, Anna W. M. *The Parents' Manual.* Rev. Ed., New York: Frederick Ungar Publishing Company, Inc., 1962.

Other Publications

Child Study Association of America
9 East 89th Street, New York, New York 10028

Behavior: The Unspoken Language of Children. Rev. Ed., 1967. 12 pp.
How to Give Your Child a Good Start, Aline B. Auerbach. Rev. Ed., 1961. 12 pp.
Some Special Problems of Children—Aged Two to Five Years, Nina Ridenour. Rev. Ed., 1966. 61 pp.
Television: How to Use It Wisely with Children, Josette Frank. Rev. Ed., 1969. 28 pp.
The One-Parent Family, Anna W. M. Wolf and Lucille Stein. 1959. 28 pp.
The Why and How of Discipline, Aline B. Auerbach. Rev. Ed., 1969. 36 pp.
What to Tell Your Child—About Birth, Death, Illness, Divorce and Other Family Crises, Helene S. Arnstein. 1964 Pocket Books. 240 pp.
What to Tell Your Child About Sex. Rev. Ed., 1968 Pocket Books. 157 pp.

Children's Bureau
Superintendent of Documents
U.S. Government Printing Office
Washington, D.C. 20402

Accidents and Children. 1963. 20 pp.
A Creative Life for Your Children, Margaret Mead. 1962. 41 pp.
A Healthy Personality for Your Child, James L. Hymes, Jr. 1952. 23 pp.
Infant Care. 1962. 108 pp.
Prenatal Care. 1962. 92 pp.
The Preschool Child Who Is Blind. 1953. 23 pp.
When Teenagers Take Care of Children: A Guide for Baby Sitters. 1964. 60 pp.
Your Baby's First Year. 1962. 28 pp.
Your Child From One to Six. 1962. 97 pp.
Your Child From 1 to 3. 1964. 20 pp.
Your Child From 3 to 4. 1967. 24 pp.

The National Association for the Education of Young Children
3110 Elm Avenue, Baltimore, Maryland 21211

Teaching the Disadvantaged Young Child, Eveline Omwake, ed. 1965.

National Association for Children Under Six
155 East Ohio Street, Chicago, Illinois 60611

Let's Play Outdoors, Katherine Read Baker. 1966. 35 pp.
Some Ways of Distinguishing a Good School or Center for Young Children. Rev., 1965. Leaflet.
"The Good Life" for Infants and Toddlers, Mary Elizabeth Keister. 1970.
What Are Kindergartens for? Anne Hoppock, 8 pp.
What Are Nursery Schools for? 8 pp.
What Is Music for Young Children? Betty Jensen Jones. 1958. 52 pp.

Enjoy Your Child—Ages 1, 2, and 3, James L. Hymes, Jr. 1950. 28 pp.
Gains for Handicapped Children, Herbert Yahraes. 1954. 28 pp.
How to Bring Up Your Child Without Prejudice, Margaret N. Young. 1965. 20 pp.
How to Help Your Handicapped Child, Samuel M. Wishik. 1955. 28 pp.
How to Tell Your Child About Sex, James L. Hymes, Jr. 1957. 28 pp.
Making the Grade as Dad, Walter Neisser. 1950. 32 pp.
Mental Health Is a Family Affair, Dallas Pratt and Jack Neher. 1949. 28 pp.
The Only Child, Eda J. LeShan. 1960. 20 pp.
Orphans of the Living: The Foster Care Crisis. 1968. 28 pp.
Serious Mental Illness in Children, Harry Milt. 1963. 28 pp.
Stepmothers Can Be Nice!, Helen Steers Burgess. 1953. 28 pp.
The Shy Child, Helen Ross. 1956. 28 pp.
Three to Six: Your Child Starts to School. James L. Hymes, Jr. 1956. 28 pp.
Time for Music—A Guide for Parents, Beatrice Landeck. 1958. 20 pp.
You and Your Adopted Child, Eda J. LeShan. 1958. 28 pp.
Your Child's Emotional Health, Anna W. M. Wolf. 1958. 28 pp.
Your New Baby, Ruth Carson. 1963. 20 pp.

Science Research Association, Inc.
57 W. Grand Avenue, Chicago, Illinois

Building Self-confidence in Children, Nina Ridenour. 1954. 48 pp.
Developing Responsibility in Children, Constance J. Foster. 1953. 48 pp.
Fears of Children, Helen Ross. 1961. 48 pp.
Helping Children Solve Problems, Ruth M. Strang. 1953.
Helping the Gifted Child, Paul Witty. 1952. 48 pp.
Self-understanding—A First Step to Understanding, William Menninger. 1951. 48 pp.
Understanding Hostility in Children, Sibylle Escalona. 1954. 48 pp.
When Children Face Crises, George J. Mohr. 1952. 48 pp.
Why Children Misbehave, Charles Leonard. 1952. 48 pp.

Filmstrips

Teaching Babies and Toddlers, Broadman Films, available at the Baptist Book Store
Teaching Twos and Threes, Broadman Films, available at the Baptist Book Store
Teaching Fours and Fives, Broadman Films, available at the Baptist Book Store
Who Am I? series, available from Scholastic Magazines, 50 W. 44 St., New York 10036 (4 filmstrips: "Nothing Is Something You Do," "The Joy of Being You," "People Packages," "Do You Believe in Wishes?")

Films

The Terrible Twos and Trusting Threes (ages and stages series), McGraw-Hill Book Company.

A close examination of the growing years between two and four

The Frustrating Fours and the Fascinating Fives (ages and stages series), McGraw-Hill Book Company.

Typical behavior at four and five

A Long Time to Grow, Part I (thirty-eight minutes) (sound), New York Film Library.

Two- and three-year-old children in daily activities at a nursery school

A Long Time to Grow, Part II (thirty-seven minutes) (sound), New York Film Library.

The spontaneous activities of four- and five-year-old children and what they find interesting in their world

The Young Child Is, Educational Improvement Center, P. O. Box 426, **Pitman, New Jersey 08071**

1. Stephen M. Joseph, *The Me Nobody Knows* (New York: Avon Books, 1969), p. 19. Used by permission.
2. *Ibid.*, p. 67.
3. *Ibid.*, p. 102.

Educational Equipment Companies
(Catalogs may be ordered.)

Childcraft Education Corporation, 964 Third Avenue, New York, New York 10022

Community Playthings, Rifton, New York 12471

Constructive Playthings, 1040 East 85th Street, Kansas City, Missouri 64131

Creative Playthings, Princeton, New Jersey 08540

(Order from stores and school distributors.)

Personal Learning Activities

Part I—Section 1

1. Observe a group of preschoolers in a church department, nursery school, or other situation with preschoolers.
   a. List some specific adult-child relationships—guidance given; evident attitudes, such as kindness, calmness, and courtesy.
   b. List kinds of behavior in child-to-child relationships—sharing, helpfulness, quarreling, selfishness, kindness.

2. Think of a preschooler you know well.
   a. Make a list of some things in his behavior of which you approve.
   b. List the behavior you dislike in the child.
   c. How do you think the child's behavior can be improved?
   d. Have you observed a difference in the child's behavior on different occasions? What do you think contributed to the difference?
   Share your findings with teachers in your department or teachers who use the same leadership guide. How do your observations compare with the author of this book?

Part I—Section 2

3. Experiment with tests on communicating trust to babies or toddlers through tone of voice, touch, and feeding. Ask a group of parents (both fathers and mothers) to participate. Use the experiment for a few days. Ask each parent to jot down notes indicating responses of the baby to the parent. Meet together and share results of the tests.

   The teachers in a Baby department at church may use the test over a period of several weeks. Each teacher should make notes on each baby's response to him or her. Discuss your findings when the experiment is completed.

   A parent may use the same plan at home to evaluate parent-child relationship.

4. During the first few months, an infant makes sounds, like *eh, ah,* and *eeh.* Do such sounds relate to language development? _____ If so, how? _____

5. Five-year-old Sue ate play dough in her church department—in fact, eating play dough seemed to be almost an obsession with her.

   The teachers often reminded Sue that the dough was to play with and not to eat, that it was not clean because all the children handled it. Sometimes Sue would cry in group time because the teacher asked for the play dough Sue held in her hand.

   In evaluation, the teachers often discussed the problem that Sue had about play dough, but they knew removing it from the room would not help Sue solve her problem.

   After about six months, as Sue was leaving the room one Sunday, she said to a teacher: "I'm trying awfully hard not to eat play dough." It was not many weeks until Sue quit eating play dough.

   Analyze the experience of Sue in relation to the basic needs. Do you think any of the following were involved in helping Sue with her problem? If so, how?

   Love
   Acceptance
   Security
   Guidance

Part I—Section 3

6. Fill in the blanks to show the development of preschoolers. (Check your answers by referring to pages 33-55.)

(a) BIRTH THROUGH ONE YEAR:

Social responses

_____

_____

Physical growth and changes

_____

_____

Emotional development

_____

_____

Language development.

_____

_____

Developmental task

_____

(b) TODDLERS:

Social responses

_____

_____

Physical growth and changes

_____

_____

Emotional development

_____

_____

Language development

_____

_____

Developmental task

_____

(c) TWO- AND THREE-YEAR-OLDS:

Social responses

_____

_____

Physical growth and changes

_____

_____

Emotional development

_____

_____

Language development

_____

_____

Developmental task

_____

(d) FOUR- AND FIVE-YEAR-OLDS:

Social responses   Physical growth and changes

_____   _____

_____   _____

Emotional development   Language development

_____   _____

_____   _____

Developmental task

_____

(e) WHAT DO YOU RECALL ABOUT SIX'S?

_____   _____

_____   _____

_____   _____

Part I—Section 4

7. Try several ways of experimenting with perception through the five senses. Use the ideas with preschoolers at church, kindergarten, nursery school, day care centers, or at home; also with adult study groups. The activities should vary in difficulty according to the skill of the group participating.

    (a) An adult will lead the group. Ask members of the group to close their eyes and listen while you make a noise. They are to guess what kind of noise.

           Use such ideas as:

               Cutting paper

               Dropping a coin

               Scratching on sandpaper

               Ringing a bell

               Clapping your hands

    (b) Show a picture to the group. Ask each person to tell what he sees in the picture, or have the group make up a story about the picture which they could tell to a two-, three-, four-, five-, or six-year-old.

(c) With adults, have several tell what event he thinks the picture depicts. Have someone list as much as possible all that is said.

(d) What activities can be used with preschoolers in developing perception?

8. Through experiences at home and church, write a desired outcome for a child you teach, using the eight areas:

God _____.

Jesus _____.

Natural world _____.

Church _____.

Bible _____.

Family _____.

Others _____.

Self _____.

Part II—Section 1

1. In a small group, give each parent or teacher a wooden inlay puzzle. Ask each person to remove the pieces and put the puzzle back together.

   Discuss the learning experiences a child may have in working a puzzle that will contribute to formal learning when he is ready for it. Examples are: concentrating, observing shapes, solving problems.

   In a large group, show a puzzle and discuss how a child uses it. Then have a discussion about learning involved in working puzzles.

   Ask: Which do you think is better for a preschooler, working a puzzle or drilling on reading words? Why?

2. Give each person in the group a magazine. Ask everyone to look through the magazines for ads that give indication of attitudes and ideas of today's adults about preschoolers.

   Analyze and discuss several of the ads. What implications do the ads show toward preschoolers?

Part II—Section 2

3. Check your knowledge of the group-living experiences for preschoolers.

	True	False
(1) Workers need to have a flexible schedule any time preschoolers are in a group.	_____	_____
(2) Memorized prayers is the best way to help the young child learn to talk to God.	_____	_____
(3) A toddler may cry when he is brought to his department because he does not want to be separated from his parents.	_____	_____
(4) Nursery school contributes to a child's social development.	_____	_____
(5) Organized game-playing is profitable in nursery school because this helps children learn to follow instructions.	_____	_____
(6) A child may be bored with kindergarten if he has attended nursery school.	_____	_____
(7) A good kindergarten needs to provide activities for cooperative play, materials for expressing creative ideas, and equipment for large-muscle development.	_____	_____
(8) A three- or four-year-old will have the same experiences in a day care center as in a good nursery school.	_____	_____
(9) A grandparent in the home can help broaden a child's understanding of family relationships.	_____	_____
(10) It is better for a child under three to have a baby-sitter in the home if the mother works.	_____	_____

4. To Discuss:

Mary was brought to the Five-Year department by the Preschool director. When Mr. William met her at the door,

Mary began screaming and did not want to go in the room.

Mary was new and the teacher realized he could not reason with her, so the teacher picked Mary up and *took* her into the room. The teacher, holding sobbing Mary in his lap, sat down by the record player and turned on the record player. Gradually, Mary's crying became more quiet and she relaxed a little.

Mr. William, still holding Mary, moved to a table nearby and picked up some play dough, then returned to the record player. The teacher took one of Mary's hands and moved her fingers around over the play dough in the teacher's hand; then he placed the dough in Mary's hand. Mary had stopped crying. The teacher moved with Mary and carefully slid Mary onto a chair at the table in the home area. Mary did not resist. She continued using the dough and gradually warmed up a little to the other preschoolers.

In her shy way, Mary participated during the remainder of the session.

This is an example of nonverbal teaching.

Do you think Mary learned anything?

If so, what?

Part II—Section 3

5. Discuss these questions:
   (1) Do you think a mother should work? Why? Why not?
   (2) What would be the best arrangement for the two-year-old if the mother works?
   (3) What effects or complications would the father's irregular absence have on the family?
   (4) What other adjustments would the family have to make?
6. Explain the need for "occupied aloneness."
7. Is there a television program, designed for children, that you find objectionable? If so, write the sponsor of the program (through your local station) and express your views.
8. For one week, keep a record of the number of hours a preschool child (or other child if you do not have a preschooler) watches television. As nearly as possible, secure a written record of the programs. Ask parents to cooperate with you.

How did the number of viewing hours compare with figures cited in Part II?

If a group uses this observation, share results at the end of the week.

Part III—Section 1

1. Observe a group of preschoolers (three or more) in any situation. Write down any problems which are evident in actions or words, such as jealousy or rivalry, fear, thumb-sucking, myths, or biting.

   If adults are present, what guidance (if any) is being given?

Part III—Section 2

2. Preschoolers may or may not develop a variety of fears. Fill in the blank space with the approximate age the fear is predominant.
   (1) Fear of being left by parents. _____
   (2) Fear of the dark. _____
   (3) Fear of loud noises, like trains, thunder, or vacuum cleaner. _____
   (4) Fear of bodily harm. _____
   (5) Fear of wild animals. _____

3. Do you think the following are good approaches to a child? Why? Why not? Discuss.
   (1) Tell a toddler that he is not big enough to feed himself.
   (2) Allow a two-year-old to have a bottle at night if he seems to need the security.
   (3) Insist that a three-year-old stay in a dark room without any light so he will get over being afraid.
   (4) If a three-year-old wets his pants while playing outdoors, keep him inside for a few days to break him of the habit.
   (5) A child should not be forced into a body of water, such as a pool or ocean.
   (6) When a three-year-old has the habit of thumb-sucking, continually remind him that he must stop.
   (7) Do not try to reason with a child while he is having a temper tantrum.

Part III—Section 3

3. Tom's dog was hit by a car and killed in front of Tom's house
   while Tom was taking a nap. What would you have done?
   - Buried the dog while Tom was asleep and let him think
     the dog was lost?
   - Helped Tom bury his dog and then rushed out to buy
     another one?
   - Helped Tom bury the dog. Listened to Tom's laments
     and grief over the death of his dog?

Part IV

1. Children differ because of:
   (1) What they _____ from their parents.
   (2) The effects of their _____. (p. 152)
2. Another term for heredity is n − t − − −.
   Another term for environment is n − − t − − −.
   (p. 152, 10-11)
3. Agree or disagree?
   (Circle "A" if you agree with the statement; circle "D" if
   you disagree.)
   (1) You can give a child too much love.   A D
   (2) Love is the child's first need.   A D
   (3) A baby knows he is loved because his parents
       tell him they love him.   A D
   (4) Love is basic in a child's spiritual growth.   A D
   (pp. 13-16)
4. A child feels he is accepted when: (Check two.)
   _____Parents like him just the way he is.
   _____Parents show they like him for what he does.
   _____He responds to rigid rules about toilet training.
   _____Parents show they love him, even when they do not
        approve of his behavior.
   (Read page 17.)
5. A child feels more secure: (Check two.)
   _____In an environment where he senses there is control.
   _____When parents give him all the things he wants.
   _____When his parents and other adults are considerate and
        well mannered.

(pp. 18-21)

6. To help a child develop a sense of trust, adults should: (Check two.)

_____Practice faith in their own lives.

_____Talk with the child about moral values.

_____Give correct answers to a child's questions.

(p. 56)

7. Agree or disagree?

(1) A child who feels rejected has difficulty developing self-respect.   A   D

(2) A child who sees himself as worthless views other people as valuable and worthy.   A   D

(3) The kind of self-image a child develops depends upon his experiences with love and acceptance.   A   D

(pp. 21-22)

8. To help a child develop independence, we should: (Check three.)

_____Never help a child with what he is trying to do.

_____Permit a child to work out his own problems.

_____Tell him he is too little for the task.

_____Allow him to do all he can for himself.

_____In the preschooler's church department, arrange materials so that they are accessible to preschoolers.

(pp. 22-25, 56-57, 153)

9. In order to have good discipline with preschoolers, adults should: (Check three.)

_____Set a lot of rigid rules.

_____Be sure the preschoolers understand limits.

_____Allow preschoolers to explore their environment uninhibited.

_____Be consistent in what they expect of a child.

_____Try to understand the reason for a child's behavior.

(pp. 25-28)

10. Agree or disagree?

(1) A child needs guidance in knowing how to be safe.   A   D

(2) A child does not need help in learning to get along with other people.   A   D

    (3) A child needs to experience success more
        often than failures.   A   D

    (4) What helps one child will also help another.   A   D

    (pp. 28-30)

11. Agree or disagree?

    (1) Through being fed when he is hungry, an
        infant begins to develop a sense of trust.   A   D

    (2) There is no need to worry about a baby's
        schedule when he is at church on Sunday.   A   D

    (3) A six-months-old baby is not aware of
        who is caring for him in a department at
        church.   A   D

    (4) A young baby senses love by the touch of
        the hands and body of those who minister
        to him.   A   D

    (5) A creeper should remain in a bed at
        church until he learns to walk.   A   D

    (6) It doesn't matter if adults use "baby talk"
        with the child before he learns to talk.   A   D

    (pp. 33-38)

12. In order to help a toddler at church, workers should:
(Check two.)

_____Be sure he does not put things in his mouth.

_____Insist that he share with others.

_____Allow the child to explore and handle things.

_____Provide some toys that are for pushing and pulling.

_____Ask the parent who brings the child to slip away
       quietly so the child won't cry.

    (pp. 38-42)

13. Agree or disagree?

    (1) Painting at an easel is too difficult a task for
        two-year-olds.   A   D

    (2) Even though a two-year-old has a short
        attention span, he needs to learn to sit in a
        group and listen to a story.   A   D

    (3) A two-year-old likes to play in a group
        situation.   A   D

    (4) Two's have vivid imaginations.   A   D

(5) Three-year-olds may be afraid to be
alone in a dark room.   A   D

(6) Three's are beginning to put into practice a
few Bible principles, such as
kindness and helpfulness.   A   D

(pp. 42-46)

14. Four- and five-year-olds:
(Check four.)

_____Have small-muscle skills so that it is easy for them
to color within lines of an outlined drawing.

_____Can cut well with scissors.

_____Improve coordination through working puzzles
and manipulating clay.

_____Are learning to share and take turns.

_____Plan ways preschoolers will use materials, like
building with blocks.

_____May experience moments of worship.

(pp. 46-53)

15. Six-year-olds have these characteristics:
(1) Very a — — — —.
(2) Like to have r — — — — — s — — — — — — y.
(3) Ready for new e — p — — — — — — — s.
(pp. 54-55)

16. The three main tasks of preschoolers are:
(1) Develop a s — — — — of t — — — —.
(2) Develop a — — — — — — — —.
(3) Develop i — — — — — — — — —.
(pp. 55-58)

17. Each child's _____ behavior will vary from that of every
other child. List two emotions of the age group you teach:

_____, _____.

(pp. 58-59)

18. These are five of the ways children learn:

(1) _____   (3) _____

(2) _____   (4) _____

(5) _____

(p. 60)

The New Church Study Course

The New Church Study Course, effective in January 1970, is based on more than three years of study and design. It offers several improvements in the Church Study Course, which began in October 1959. At that time three courses previously promoted by the Sunday School Board were merged: the Sunday School Training Course, the Graded Training Union Study Course, and the Church Music Training Course. Principles and methods books of the Woman's Missionary Union and the Brotherhood Commission were added in October 1961 and January 1967, respectively.

The New Church Study Course offers increased flexibility in meeting the needs of Southern Baptists. It provides courses of varying length and difficulty, varied formats and types of course materials, additional types of credit, and improved organization of courses.

The New Church Study Course consists of two types of courses: the Christian Development Courses for all church members and the Christian Leadership Courses for church leaders. Courses are organized into subject areas.

The purpose of Christian Development Courses is to provide courses of study which will help church members grow toward maturity in Christian living and competence in Christian service. These courses offer more comprehensive, advanced, and varied learning experiences in subject areas of a church's educational program that can be provided through curriculum periodicals. Tests and exercises, credits, and diplomas of achievement which help church members measure their progress in developing needed knowledge, understanding, and skills are included in some courses. Units of instruction are provided for Preschoolers and Children. These are designed to reinforce foundational learnings. Materials which churches may use in recognizing the participation of Children in these units are available from Baptist Book Stores.

Christian Leadership Courses provide a comprehensive series of courses into subject areas dealing with knowledge, understanding, and skills needed for effective church leadership. Tests and exercises and credits and diplomas to help leaders measure their growth in leadership ability are included in some courses. The Christian Leadership Courses are the primary source for leadership training materials prepared by the agencies cooperating in the New Church Study Course. Courses of both types are designed to be effective for individual and class study. Learning aids, study guides, and teaching guides are available for some courses. Credits are granted to Youth and Adults for reading, individual study, and class study.

The New Church Study Course is promoted by the Sunday School Board, 127 Ninth Avenue, North, Nashville, Tennessee 37234, through the departments in the Church Services and Materials Division; by the Woman's Missionary Union, 600 North Twentieth Street, Birmingham, Alabama 35203; by the Brotherhood Commission, 1548 Poplar Avenue, Memphis, Tennessee 38104; and by the respective departments in the state conventions affiliated with the Southern Baptist Convention.

A record of all credits and diplomas earned should be maintained in each church.

Detailed information about the course and the system of credits, diplomas, and record keeping is available from the agencies listed above.

Forms for keeping records may be ordered from any Baptist Book Store.

The New Church Study Course
Requirements for Credit

This book is the text for course 6101 of subject area "Understanding Work with Age Level and Special Groups in a Church" in the Christian Leadership Courses of the New Church Study Course. If credit is desired for this course through class study, individual study, or reading, the following requirements must be met:

I. Classwork

1. This course is designed for ten (10) hours of class study and carries four credits for such usage. If the course is studied in a class setting of less than ten (10) hours, the following criteria apply:

   (1) Seven and one half ($7\frac{1}{2}$) class hours—three (3) credits

   (2) Five (5) class hours—two (2) credits

   (3) Two and one half class hours—one (1) credit

   The teacher will indicate the length of the class and the number of credits to be granted on Form 151, Request for Course Credit (revised).

   For courses in which laboratory experience or practice is desirable, two (2) hours of such guided experience may be substituted as one (1) hour of class time, provided at least.

178

half of the required hours are actually spent in classwork.

2. A class member who attends all class sessions and completes the reading of the book as directed by the teacher will not be required to do any written work for credit.

3. A class member who is absent from one or more sessions must complete the required exercises or questions in the "Personal Learning Activities" section on all chapters he misses. In such a case, he must turn in his paper by the date the teacher sets (usually within ten days following the last class). Also, he must certify that he has read the book.

4. The teacher should request credits for himself. A person who teaches a course for Youth or Adults (in any subject area) will be granted the same number of credits as class members. The teacher of an approved unit of study for Preschoolers and Children will be granted two credits in course 6101 in subject area 61. Request credits on Form 151.

5. The church training director, or the person designated by the church, should complete Form 151, Request for Course Credit (revised), and forward it after completion of the class to the Church Study Course Awards Office, 127 Ninth Avenue, North, Nashville, Tennessee 37234.

II. Individual Study

1. A person who wishes to complete this course without attending class sessions may receive full credit by certifying that he has read the book and has completed all exercises or questions in the "Personal Learning Activities" section.

2. Students may find profit in studying the text together, but individual papers are required. Carbon copies or duplicates of the answers cannot be accepted.

3. The work required for individual study credit should be turned in for checking to the church training director or to the person designated by the church to administer the New Church Study Course. Form 151, Request for Course Credit (revised), must be used in requesting credit. It is to be forwarded by the church training director, or the person designated by the church, to the Church Study Course Awards Office, 127 Ninth Avenue, North, Nashville, Tennessee 37234.

III. Reading Credit

1. A person may receive one credit toward the diploma on which he is working by reading this book.
2. Upon completion of the reading, he must complete Form 151, Request for Course Credit (revised). He should give the completed form to the church training director or to the person designated by his church to be responsible for administering the New Church Study Course.
3. The church training director, or the person designated by the church, will see that the request is completed, signed, and forwarded to the Church Study Course Awards Office, 127 Ninth Avenue, North, Nashville, Tennessee 37234.

IV. Awards and Records

Two copies of the course credit awards form will be sent by the Study Course Awards Office to the church. The original copy should be filed in the church training record and the duplicate given to the individual.

QUESTIONS I HAVE

COMMENTS TO REMEMBER